Best Wishes

Bernard Cadbury.

WENTWORTH

Wentworth

WENTWORTH CLUB LIMITED

EDITOR'S ACKNOWLEDGEMENTS

This book could not have been completed without the help and cooperation of many people. John Robertson, Managing Director of Golf World Ltd, gave access readily to the valuable files at *Golf Illustrated* allowing Dave Cannon and his team at Allsport the facility to do much reproduction photography.

Many of my fellow golf writers who have enjoyed a long and happy relationship with the Club assisted in telling the story of Wentworth over the past 70 years and in recalling the drama and excitement of the World Match-play Championship since 1964.

Many members of the Club provided considerable help and encouragement, too, especially on the historical front for which I was most grateful.

Along with my diligent colleague John Youé, the designer of the book, and the always meticulous Laurence Viney who played such an important part in ensuring editorial integrity, I should like to record my grateful thanks to Willy Bauer and the always cooperative staff of Wentworth Club for all their assistance over the past eighteen months. My thanks to everyone who helped in any way in the publication of this celebration of Wentworth's 70 years but finally and certainly not least, I want to acknowledge a special debt of gratitude to former Club Secretary Richard Doyle-Davidson whom the Club wisely put in charge of the project. His knowledge of Club affairs was invaluable but even more important to us all was his always unstinting cheerfulness and enthusiasm.

Renton Laidlaw
September 1993

ISBN 0-9521595-0-3

Production Consultant: Laurence Viney
Printed by White Crescent Press, Luton
Bound by Green Street Bindery, Oxford

CONTENTS

HRH THE DUKE OF EDINBURGH

Everyone who has ever played at the Wentworth Club knows and appreciates the quality of its courses. They also know that the Club has either initiated or hosted almost every major national and international golfing event.

Founded only 70 years ago, the Club may not be among the pioneers of the game, but what it lacks in antiquity it makes up for in quality and initiative. I have several special reasons to be grateful to the Club. Some years ago the Duke of Edinburgh 100 Golfing Society was formed to help raise funds for the Duke of Edinburgh Award Scheme. The Club is based at Wentworth.

Golf has always been one of the choices in the Recreation Section of the Award Scheme and it is at the Wentworth Club that qualifying participants in nine regional events play for the Golden Putter, donated by the Club.

I think the Club also deserves to be in the Guinness Book of Records for naming one of its courses after someone who never got beyond learning to play the game!!

This book shows that the Wentworth Club has crammed a great deal into its first 70 years, but by the time it reaches its Centenary, I am sure that a lot more interesting material will have been added.

1993

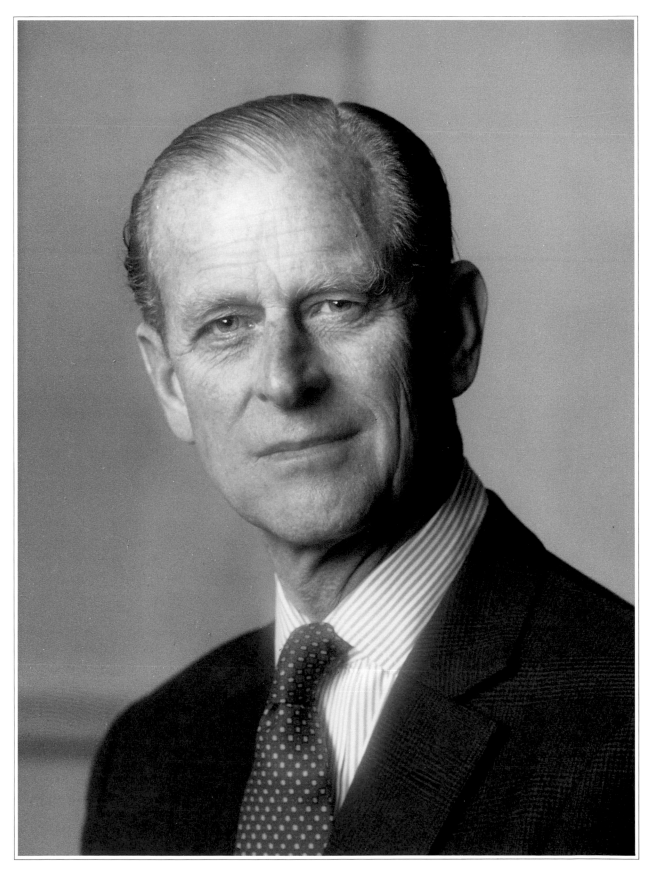

Introduction

ELLIOTT BERNERD

When I first commissioned this publication to coincide with the opening of the refurbished clubhouse, I had no idea what an enthralling and absorbing book it would turn out to be. It captures many facets of Wentworth since its earliest inception and is interspersed with the right blend of anecdotes and, at times, controversial comment. It gives an interesting viewpoint not just on Wentworth throughout its illustrious history but also an insight into the role it has played in the development of the game.

This book will be treasured by Club members for many years to come, and those golfers who prefer match-play golf will enjoy the selection of some of the finest matches ever played between the greats of this golfing age.

I was quite amazed by the depth of research which has been carried out and my grateful thanks go to all our friends – the golfing writers, who have contributed to this excellent work.

It also makes us realize that each succeeding generation of owners and members of Wentworth have left things better for their successors. This surely is the essence of a great golf club whose reputation improves with every decade.

CLUB CHAIRMAN

An Historical Perspective

RENTON LAIDLAW

Walter George Tarrant's success in developing quality housing around a well-designed golf course at St George's Hill near Weybridge just after the turn of the century, prompted him to look for suitable land where he could repeat the exercise. He discovered Wentworth.

Today, many golf course developments around the world cannot even be contemplated without the financial assistance of a housing development to provide the necessary cash flow to enable the course to be built. Tarrant, a builder and craftsman, was ahead of his time in this respect at Wentworth. He was fortunate that 70 years ago there was the good land available and planning laws were less restrictive than today, both of which helped him turn his vision into reality.

Had it not been for Tarrant, Wentworth would not exist today and but for his friendship with Harry Colt the Club would not rejoice in owning not one but two of the finest courses in England, never mind the stockbroker belt of Surrey. A more modern third was completed recently by John Jacobs, Gary Player and Bernard Gallacher to a standard of which Colt would have approved.

Sadly, the history of the Wentworth Club is incomplete, books and papers having been lost during the Second World War when the Club was requisitioned by the army. In addition, other notes, ledgers and artifacts have been permanently mislaid by less than careful Club officials over the years. Yet the beginnings of the Club, which owes much to the drive and enthusiasm of Tarrant, and the history of the land on which the original courses were built, are well enough documented.

What, I wonder, would Tarrant think of Wentworth today? How proud would he be of its international reputation? How satisfied would he be that his bold plan, ahead of its time, for a mix of golf courses and houses in a superb wooded, heathland setting, had turned out so well and had so successfully stood the test of time? Delighted on all three counts, I fancy, but not surprised because the emphasis from the start was on quality – two excellent courses and Tarrant homes so well built that he was proud to put his monogram on the sides of the buildings.

In the early years of the century when, despite the horrors of the First World War, the golf course building boom in Britain was at its peak – a boom that is being mirrored on the Continent today in France, Spain, Germany and Sweden – courses were often built near to railway lines. One line ran from London's Waterloo Station to Reading, Guildford and Windsor with a junction at Virginia Water, the village closest to the parcel of land that Tarrant set his eyes on for possible development in the St George's Hill style.

Thus, unlike the Sunningdale Club, another of the great Surrey sand belt courses just a few miles away, Wentworth had a nearby station that was ready and waiting. Sunningdale members had to persuade one of their own who happened to be an important figure on the Railway Company Board to build a station nearby to make it easier for members without motor cars to get to and from their course.

The Wentworth site was perfect – softly rolling countryside which Tarrant knew he could develop without causing any lasting damage to

Line drawing of the Mansion 'Wentworth' before it was adapted to become the first clubhouse

the area. Indeed, he was sure he could enhance the site in many ways and certainly provide an enjoyable location for people with money to set up house and play golf, a gentle, healthy game noted for its sportsmanship and gentlemanliness. It was the perfect mix.

Wentworth was not the original name of the area. It was the name of one small parcel of land on the bigger Podenhall Estate. Today, the name Wentworth describes the whole area and Podenhall (now Portnall) refers to one location on the estate.

The courses are built on land with which Chertsey Abbey endowed a small nunnery at Broomhall near Sunningdale soon after the Norman Conquest. Later, yeoman farmers took it over and in the 18th century, noblemen and professional people, who even then had an eye for good investment, bought it up.

One such speculator was Church of Ireland dignitary John Jebb, Dean of Cashel. In 1761 he bought up land at Podenhall originally owned by London businessman Robert Lord who had passed it on to his daughter Elizabeth. She had married Lieutenant-General Thomas Wentworth whose name became associated with the area in preference to Podenhall.

In 1782 John Jebb bought the land on which the Dormy House now stands. It was these two purchases, 21 years apart, that provided the ground which, over 100 years later, Tarrant would hand over to designer Harry Colt to turn into the East and West golf courses.

After John Jebb died, his son David took over the property but he sold off much of it . One buyer was Culling Charles Smith back from India where his family had had dealings with the East India Company and who had married well. His wife was Lady Anne Fitzroy, sister of the future Duke of Wellington. On the land he bought from Jebb was Virginia Farm where he built a house in the fashionable Gothic style with ramparts. He called it Wentworths and lived there for 40 years. A century later Tarrant would use this house as the Wentworth clubhouse. With much of his finances tied up in a Trust, Culling Smith was forced to sell off Wentworths in 1842 but the original family plaque – a shield showing the arms of the Smiths and the Welleseys – survives to this day on the newly built, redesigned clubhouse.

Culling Smith sold to Sir George Caulfield. In 1854 he sold it on to the exiled Spanish military man Ramon Cabrera, the Count de Morella, and his wife Marianne who was the daughter of a wealthy London barrister and heiress to his considerable fortune. Although Cabrera's reputation as man and soldier left something to be desired, Marianne bore him two sons and three daughters and continued to run the estate with the help of one unmarried daughter for 40 years after his death. The Countess's father had owned considerable property and during the period in which she ran things at Wentworths she embarked on such an ambitious expansion policy that by the time of her death at the age of 95 she had increased the original 300 acres of the estate to 1,500 acres. The golf courses are built on 500 acres of the

Miss Seed is receiving her pupils, for the duration of the war, at
"Wentworth,"
Virginia Water,
Surrey.

The house is situated a mile and a half from Virginia Water Station, on the L. & S.W.R., about 40 minutes by train from Waterloo Station.

The French Resident Staff and the general life and study of the household are practically the same as in Paris.

Special Lessons can be continued as before with professors in town.

A certificated teacher of Domestic Economy, First-Aid, and Home Nursing has been added to the Resident Staff.

Miss Seed will be glad to see or hear from parents at 60 Gloucester Place, London W.1, until April the 8th, and later at "Wentworth"

During the First World War the mansion housed Miss Seed's school which had been evacuated from Paris

old Podenhall Estate which she bought from the descendents of Thomas Day, a wealthy philanthropist who had invested in the area at the same time as John Jebb was buying up land.

So by 1915, a few years before Tarrant began looking around for land on which to build a second St George's Hill, the land on which the clubhouse and golf courses could be built was neatly tied up in one package owned by the surviving spinster daughter Ada Cabrera. Happily for Tarrant, she did not want it.

In 1920 she attempted to auction off the whole lot and failed. A few small acreages were disposed of but nothing substantial. Tarrant did not have the money to buy the whole estate but, after shrewd negotiating with Ada, struck a deal to buy the land in stages over a period of ten years. The total purchase price of the first package of Wentworth land amounting to nearly 200 acres, with 45 acres of the Portnall Park estate which was bounded on three sides by Wentworth, was £42,000.

Tarrant had achieved his goal and set up the first Wentworth Golf Club board. It comprised himself, Harry Colt, who would design the courses, Evan Robert Davies and Edwin John Elliott who would act as Secretary.

Wentworth, which would play such an important part in the developing history of golf in Britain, was off and running. But at a loss. In the year from November 1924 to December 1925 when the first course – now known as the East – was completed but the second course, which the committee felt was costing a ludicrous £5,000 to build, had not been finished, the Club's finances showed a running costs deficit of £4,200 despite assets of £62,000 and despite having signed up 584 members in the first year of operation – a considerable achievement considering that there were already several well-established courses in the area. In those days, memberships were easier to

April 10th, 1920.   Supplement to COUNTRY LIFE.   XV.

KNIGHT, FRANK & RUTLEY AND WALTON & LEE
LONDON, EDINBURGH, GLASGOW AND ASHFORD, KENT.

BY DIRECTION OF MISS CABRERA.

SURREY
VIRGINIA WATER:

ADJACENT TO VIRGINIA WATER AND SUNNINGDALE STATIONS RESPECTIVELY, 21 MILES FROM HYDE PARK CORNER.
THE FREEHOLD, MANORIAL, RESIDENTIAL AND SPORTING ESTATE, KNOWN AS

WENTWORTH
extending to an area of about

1,808 ACRES

THE MANSION.

And comprising the Mansion of "WENTWORTH," situated in a well-timbered park, with lake and pinewoods, and containing seven reception, billiard, 22 bed and dressing rooms, and four bathrooms. Two other Residences, "KENWOLDE COURT" and "MERLEWOOD," occupying commanding positions, and containing four reception, eighteen bedrooms, and four reception and twelve bedrooms respectively. THE MANOR OF TROTTSWORTH. The home and two other farms, smaller holdings, and over 20 cottages. Extensive areas of Pinewoods interspersed with open and undulating lands clad with bracken and heather, and watered by small streams. Residential sites. Sandy soil. Fine views. VACANT POSSESSION of the MANSION and FARMS. CAPITAL SPORTING with pheasants, wild duck, hares, and rabbits. HUNTING with the Garth. GOLF at Sunningdale.

THE PRINCIPAL LOTS INCLUDE:

LOT 14. "Wentworth" . . 357 ACRES. | LOT 32. "Kenwolde Court" 15 ACRES. | LOT 9. Trottsworth Farm. . 255 ACRES.
„ 33. "Merlewood" . . 24 „ | „ 22. Warren Farm . . 335 „ | „ 15. Pinewoods and Heathland 445 „

TO BE OFFERED FOR SALE BY AUCTION, AS A WHOLE OR IN LOTS, AT AN EARLY DATE (UNLESS PREVIOUSLY SOLD). Particulars of Sale, with plan and views, price 2s. 6d. each. Solicitor, A. DALLAS-BRETT, Esq., Egham, Surrey; Resident Agent, W. PAICE, Esq., Wentworth Cottage, Virginia Water, Surrey. Auctioneers, Messrs. KNIGHT, FRANK & RUTLEY, 20, Hanover Square, W. 1.

Notice of sale of 1,808 acres of the Wentworth Estate in 1920. Note the 20 Hanover Square address of Knight, Frank and Rutley, still the same today

come by than they are today!

Much of the purchase price was raised by selling £100 debentures offering a dividend of five per cent per annum. Clearly, there were plenty of investors who were as enthusiastic as Tarrant was about the potential of the Wentworth development.

The developer kept firm control of Club expenditure while building and selling his luxury homes and constructing the courses to Colt's designs. At one stage, he pointed out to the committee that in order to make £8 profit in the dining room it was necessary to serve 160 lunches or 320 teas! Style was always the keynote. Thus, Tarrant and his committee only agreed to have a booklet prepared about the Club and its courses on the condition that the editorial was supplied by Bernard Darwin, the respected golf correspondent of *The Times*. Darwin was the grandson of Charles Darwin, author of *The Origin of Species*, and himself an accomplished golfer.

Designer Colt, a member of the Royal & Ancient, a former Secretary at Sunningdale and an international golfer who in his heyday as a competitor had won many cups and trophies, left the

Walter George Tarrant

MAN WITH A VISION

The Wentworth estate was the brainchild of Walter George Tarrant, born in 1875 the son of a Portsmouth policeman. Through hard work and intuition he became a builder of quality homes in Byfleet.

Wentworth, modelled on the earlier St George's Hill Estate developed by Tarrant, was further proof that he cared about maintaining the high standard of what he built and had a sensitive regard for the amenities in the estate in which the houses were being built. The houses were constructed to the highest specifications with Tarrant incorporating his WGT monogram in the brickwork – a sign which estate agents still use today as a hallmark of quality. Although he did not design the golf courses, it was Tarrant and his men who built them.

A burly, bearded figure who bore a striking resemblance to King Edward VII, Tarrant also designed and built almost entirely from wood a gigantic triplane –

bigger than a Second World War Flying Fortress. He called it the Tarrant Tabor. It was intended to be used for bombing raids on Berlin during the First World War with the longer term plan of converting it for use as a passenger plane. Unfortunately, on its very first trial the plane crashed even before take-off, killing three crew members.

A supporter of good causes – young people, war veterans and sports clubs all benefitted from his generosity – he was a popular figure in the neighbourhood and a forceful campaigner in local politics, too. In 1931 his firm, like many businesses suffered in the Great Depression and only narrowly escaped bankruptcy but his natural enterprise allowed him to survive and, after a spell of farming and market gardening in Hampshire, he moved to Cardiganshire and Cwymstwyth where he eventually died in 1942.

Wentworth is his memorial.

PERCY HIGGS

Wentworth Board in 1926. This came as no surprise. He seldom involved himself as closely with a club as he had at Wentworth and it was clear that his other commissions were preventing him from devoting time to shaping policy at Wentworth.

He had been redesigning Blackmoor in Hampshire. He had redesigned the Muirfield course of the Honourable Company of Edinburgh Golfers which had become outdated as equipment, most notably the golf ball, had been improved. He was working on the course at Moor Park some 25 miles away, north west of London, when he sent his letter of resignation to the Club. It was accepted with understanding by Tarrant and the other members of the committee but with considerable regret as well.

Helped by a substantial profit from the Club's wine account, the 1925 deficit was halved in 1926, and the value of the assets showed a 20 per cent improvement. By 1927, after another influx of members following the opening of the second course – later an eighteen hole short course would be added – the Club began to operate at a small profit and the ballroom was in continuous demand for dances, parties and special functions featuring professional artistes.

With the two main courses in play the members began to describe them as the East – the original course – and the West, later to be known as the Burma Road because German prisoners of war from nearby Egham camp were put to work clearing all the vegetation that had grown up on the last six holes when the course was closed

Certificate for the £100 debentures issued by W G Tarrant Ltd in 1924. One of the signatories is Harry Colt

during the Second World War.

In the late 1920s the Club prided itself, too, on offering more favourable daily rates than its nearby rival Sunningdale. The contrast between Sunningdale and Wentworth was considerable. Wentworth, with tennis and squash courts and later a swimming pool, was always more than a golf club; it was the prototype of a country club. Sunningdale could offer none of these facilities and did not want to.

A day ticket at Wentworth, offering as much golf as you could play, cost five shillings (25 pence in today's money) during the week and five shillings at weekends. This was the cost of one round at Sunningdale!

Wentworth was also ahead of its time in the way it handled its business with the Club Professional. The first was George Duncan, a Scotsman who was a personal friend of Colt. When he left in 1929, the Club bought all Duncan's stock and offered John Aitken the job on a unique basis. The Club would pay Aitken a retainer and give him one third of the profits from the equipment sold in the shop, the repairs he did to clubs and the lessons he gave. The Club would keep the remaining two thirds. If he made a success of the job, provision was made for him to earn a bonus.

By the end of 1929, the assets were worth £81,000 and Wentworth was clearly a success. As early as 1925, Tarrant and his board had decided that, in a bid to attract more members, they should attempt to give Wentworth an international reputation. The Club was advertised on transatlantic ships and in America. In the early 1930s the Club embarked on a sales campaign in London to help boost finances stretched by initial capital costs and the cost of playing the first Curtis Cup match on the East course. Representatives visited such clubs as the Conservative Club, the Bath Club, the Army and Navy, and the Cavalry Club to see whether their members might be interested in associating themselves with Wentworth and playing or joining on very favourable terms.

By 1931, Tarrant indicated that he would be leaving the Board of Wentworth Golf Club because he claimed that his own building business was being ignored. He was happy, however, to complete any unfinished business and only too willing to quote for any new business on which the Club might embark at a future date. In fact, he did not cut himself off from the Club because he formed Wentworth Estates Ltd to own and manage the Club. As reluctantly as they had let Colt go, the Board accepted Tarrant's resignation and in August 1931 the man who had founded and fostered the Wentworth Club stood down. It was, as Alick Watt explained in his excellently researched history of the Club, the end of an era.

In 1932, by which time Wentworth had 1,150 members, the Curtis Cup heightened international awareness of the Club. At the same time, committee activities decreased as a result, one suspects, of the departure of Mr Tarrant, the driving force for the first few years.

The clubhouse in 1928

Nevertheless, Club activities continued, matches were played and tournaments staged, including one in 1934 sponsored by Messrs Hardy Brothers of Alnwick in Northumberland who had showrooms in Pall Mall.

The event was unique. Hardy Brothers, who had made cane fishing rods since 1872, had developed a cane golf club shaft made up of twelve pieces of wedge-shaped bamboo as an alternative to hickory. Six of the parts were glued together to form a slender shaft which was then covered by a further six pieces. The club was known as the Palakona and Alf Padgham won the tournament playing the revolutionary equipment. Many sets were sold but sadly the Palakona club, now a highly prized collector's item, was totally eclipsed a few years later by the steel shaft.

In 1935, Ada Cabrera who had played her part in the development of the Wentworth Club, died. Her estate and effects were valued at nearly £250,000 when her will was published.

By the outbreak of the Second World War, the Club membership list had swollen to 1,480, two thirds of whom were active golfers. They had few criticisms of the courses which had been further improved by the clearing of scrub and the piping of water to the seventeenth and eighteenth greens of the West course. The clubhouse had been renovated and restored in part too and, as part of a refurbishment programme, a new bar had been built but the outbreak of war led to the Wentworth Estate being requisitioned by the military.

Only the East course was maintained to what was described as 'customary standard' on which golf continued to be played throughout the war years on a limited basis. In order to prevent German gliders from landing on the fairway at the sixteenth hole of the East, two new wing bunkers were built. They are still in play today.

It was in early 1943 that Colonel G W Parkinson bought the whole of the Tarrant investment but, unfortunately, the colonel was killed the same year and his widow, Mrs L B Parkinson, was left with the reponsibility of looking after his affairs. Later that year, Sir Lindsay Parkinson & Co Ltd under the chairmanship of Mr A E (Teddy) Parkinson – Sir Lindsay's nephew – bought the estate from Mrs L B Parkinson (no relation to the new owners) and became a Director and later Chairman of the Club, a post he held for 30 years.

Teddy Parkinson gave the Club's Trustees a guarantee that should they ever decide to dispose of their shares in Wentworth Club Ltd, the Trustees would be given first option to purchase the Club on behalf of the Members. This guarantee proved to be controversially ineffective later, when to circumvent this clause, the share capital of Sir Lindsay Parkinson & Co Ltd, which owned Wentworth Club Ltd was acquired by Leonard Fairclough Ltd.

By 1947, the East and West courses had been brought back to full playing condition and nine holes of the original eighteen on the short course were brought back into play. Wentworth's reputation as a venue for top golfing events continued to grow. The staging of the

The swimming pool in the 1930s

Aerial view of the clubhouse and adjoining buildings about 1953

Dunlop 2000 tournament in 1950 was so successful that the Club Executive were confident enough to feel that they could stage the 1953 Ryder Cup for the Professional Golfers' Association. Amateur and professional tournaments featuring men and women were commonplace at the Club which had become one of Britain's most used venues. The 1952 Daks event was the first to be televised in Britain and the Ballantines tournament was one of the first in which the big ball was compulsory for all competitors.

The success the Club made of holding the Ryder Cup match was no surprise to anyone even though the man handling it, Major Peter Roscow, had been Club Secretary for less than a year. It had not all been plain sailing at the Club, of course. Because of the War, membership had dropped to 941 and the Club, constantly making improvements to the clubhouse and courses, often operated at an annual loss. This was later changed by Chairman Parkinson insisting that more realistic fees be charged.

In 1956, the Club minutes recount the concern of the Board about the catering profits being adversely affected by rising wages, the pensions bill and the cost of providing staff food! Increases were made in all charges, leaving the visitor's day ticket with lunch and tea at £1 7s 6d (£1.37 in today's money).

The Club appointed its first President and Vice President in 1957, Admiral of the Fleet Sir Charles Forbes and Commander R St John RN. The same year, Mrs Parkinson was elected an honorary

When the Wentworth Club went to war

While Wentworth's West course is known round the world, another unique feature at the Club is hardly ever spoken about – the emergency underground headquarters built during the Second World War and used by such as Montgomery and Eisenhower. The Club and many of the houses on the estate had been requisitioned by the Army at the outbreak of war in 1939. While no records can be found that give details of when or how it was built, we do know why thanks to the painstaking research done for the Club by John Wenzel, former curator of the much better known underground Cabinet rooms in London.

In 1941, it was decided that it would be prudent to build a command post outside the city as an alternative HQ for the Home Forces because of the regular and heavy bombing raids on central London. But that is only half the story.

It seems that General Sir Alan Brooke, Chief of the Imperial General Staff from late 1941, (later to become Viscount Alanbrooke) had another reason for wanting to move lock, stock and barrel to the country. His underground headquarters in Whitehall was so close to that of the Prime Minister, Winston Churchill, that he wanted alternative accommodation as far from central London as possible in order to avoid political interference in his command, especially by Churchill who was a difficult taskmaster. Wentworth, a top secret Army camp during the war, was an ideal alternative to the Cabinet War Rooms and was a much more effective

command post, offering far greater resources and far fewer security problems. Later, it would be used by Montgomery's 21st Army Group and there is more than a suggestion that D-Day was planned in the Wentworth bunker.

An added advantage of the location – and a further excuse to move out of the London base – was the elimination of the problems with communications that could be caused by the nightly bombing of central London. The city headquarters was secure from the raids but the communications network from the London bunker was not. At Wentworth Alan Brooke's lines of communication avoided London altogether.

The 45-foot deep subterranean control centre was constructed with walls of bomb-proof concrete that were 6 feet thick. At the base of a 30-foot slope leading from the main entrance there was a 400-yard corridor with offices off it on both sides, now all in a state of disrepair. When it was abandoned by the Army, they took away everything including the floorboards!

In 1943, golf for the general public was out at Wentworth although officers based there could become honorary members on the payment of 1s 0d (5p in today's money) and a charge of 3d a round.

For 4s 0d a night Army officers could stay at the Georgian-style Dormy House, the mansion in the original 180-acre Portnall estate that was swallowed up by Walter George Tarrant when he conceived Wentworth in the early 1920s.

A War Office memo dated 16 November 1940, stated that in order to allow officers to spend short periods in the country, accommodation had been member as were the Korean ambassador and his wife, underlining still further the international reputation of the Club.

The high profile the Club enjoyed in the late 1950s and early 1960s – what Alick Watt in his history calls 'the vintage years' – saw membership increase again to 1,600, just 100 short of the limit set by the Club.

The disruption of members' opportunities to play caused by the staging of tournaments and the large number of visiting societies, was a niggling problem at Wentworth, so the Club compared notes with The Berkshire and Royal Mid-Surrey, clubs which also operated with two courses. In 1966, The Berkshire had 600 members using the facilities, Royal Mid-Surrey 725, both well below the Wentworth

arranged in six rooms at the Dormy House. All rooms had separate bathrooms and constant hot water. A comfortable dining anteroom had been specially furnished for the officers enjoying brief periods of leave away from the rigours of war at a cost of 3s 0d a night to cover the cost of furniture hire, the provision of clean sheets and towels with a 2s 0d a day charge for their mess with a bar operating at the prevailing mess prices!

The wartime warren, the Club, the grounds and most of the homes on the estate which had been requisitioned, were heavily fortified. The grounds bristled with gun emplacements, prefabricated huts and ammunition dumps.

Former special police constable John Hammond, one of the few locals ever allowed inside the top secret Army camp recalled in the Surrey Herald: 'It was all very hush-hush. Without a pass you could not get anywhere near the camp. There were guards everywhere with a major sentry post at the Club entrance.'

In his Surrey Herald article, Graeme Bryan,who did much research on the undergound HQ, reported that there was one major diplomatic incident at Wentworth during the war. General Leopold Sikorski, the leader of the Polish government in exile, unwittingly leased a home in the middle of the camp from a house owner who had not been told that his house had already been requisitioned by the British!

Quartermaster-General Sir Walter Venning was anxious not to offend the Polish General and pointed out, in a note to General Sir Alan Brooke, that the difficulties of dealing with the situation were 'fairly

considerable'. Brooke saw no difficulties at all. He wrote back stating unequivocally that Sikorski should not be allowed to take up residence and he never did.

Richard Doyle-Davidson and John Wenzel explore the underground bunker

membership figure which was then reduced to a maximum of 1,000 by natural wastage adding greater exclusivity in the process.

With the Club so well established, the minutes at this time deal to a large extent with the normal day-to-day running of a proprietary Club, one run commercially and profitably by the owner – effectively Teddy Parkinson who lived above the shop, as it were, in a house on the eighteenth fairway of the West course. It is important to remember that at no time in the Club's history has Wentworth ever been run, like most clubs are, by the members. Not that the Wentworth members did not get a good deal from the Parkinson family. The members were always consulted and their views sought by owners who were keen to maintain the clubhouse and courses to a high standard within the available budget. When *The Sunday Times* golf correspondent Henry Longhurst, as respected a golf commentator after the 1939-45 War as Bernard Darwin had been in the 1920s, was asked to write an article in a publicity brochure for the Club, his payment was a case of whisky!

So many events were now being staged at Wentworth that the green-keeping staff were kept busy preparing the West course in particular for important competitions. One year, Wentworth staged five major tournaments in the first six months of the year all very successfully but it did stretch the resources of the staff. Dai Rees, the fiery Welshman who captained the Great Britain & Ireland team to success in the 1957 Ryder Cup at Lindrick during his long and exceptionally meritorious career, described the crowds at the 1962 Dunlop Masters at Wentworth as the largest he had ever seen for a sponsored event. He commented that the arrangements for the players and the facilities provided for the paying public were bigger and better than ever. This was the time, of course, when Binnie Clark, forward thinking tournament director for the Gallagher cigarette company one of whose brands was Senior Service, thought up the idea of building a tented village offering golf fans the opportunity to lunch, buy golfing gear or browse in comfort. He pioneered this idea with his event at Dalmahoy in Edinburgh. Later augmented by hospitality units, the tented village idea quickly caught on.

Wentworth was so popular a venue that it was no surprise when Mark McCormack, a young thrusting Cleveland lawyer asked the Club to host the inaugural World Match-play – an event still played at the Club today. He had seen and capitalized on the opportunity to manage golfers such as Arnold Palmer. McCormack's International Management Group now manages hundreds of clients and not only in golf – the Pope was once a client.

Over the years the debenture holders – those who had inititally supported the Club in 1924 – had enjoyed subsidized golf at Wentworth. Their subscriptions were maintained at a low rate and they had the right to invite, free of charge, three guests daily. Their cheap golf may also have enabled some of them to 'double up' by joining nearby Sunningdale or The Berkshire. This advantageous situation ended in

1974 when all debentures were redeemed or, at least, as many as could be. Many bond holders never made themselves known to the Board which was still chaired by Teddy Parkinson although his long term in that seat was coming to an end.

In 1974 the minutes refer to 'the new relationship' with Leonard Fairclough & Co Ltd which had bought out the share issue of Sir Lindsay Parkinson & Co – a transaction that did not invoke the guarantee made to the members by Teddy Parkinson to offer them first refusal if the Club was sold. The Club changed hands because it was part of a large company deal, not because the Club alone had been put up for sale by its owners. Indeed, Fairclough was surprised to discover that it had inherited a golf club as famous as Wentworth!

It was during the Fairclough era that the Great Wood, on which the Edinburgh course would later be built, was purchased – a forward thinking move that greatly benefitted the Club. There were niggling problems, however, and at one stage the members did try to buy Wentworth but Fairclough was not interested in disposing of such a valuable asset. To reassure members that it did have a commitment to the Club it signed up Richard Doyle-Davidson, Secretary of the Formby Club in Lancashire, as General Manager and he is still much involved with the Club today.

In the early 1980s Fairclough amalgamated with William Press and formed a holding company, AMEC plc, and it was AMEC that sold the Club to Elliott Bernerd's Chelsfield property company in order to raise captital for its core business in 1988. AMEC had decided to get out of the leisure industry in which Wentworth was its only interest, but not before the company had embarked on an exciting £6 million plan to knock down and rebuild the clubhouse.

The deal with Chelsfield was concluded quickly, AMEC taking the view that, as with the Parkinson-Fairclough sale, it could dispose of Wentworth without having to give the members first option to buy. In days rather than months the sale was negotiated for £32 million.

Today, the Club enjoys a well deserved reputation in world golf and in recent years many improvements have been completed, not least the total rebuilding and refurbishment of the old clubhouse behind the original façade of the castellated home built by Culling Smith nearly two centuries earlier.

Over the years, Wentworth has remained a venue of beauty and tranquillity where, despite its proximity to Heathrow Airport – the busiest in Europe and nonexistent in Tarrant's day – it is still possible to escape from the hurly-burly and the pressures of modern day living and enjoy a walk in the unspoilt country with a set of golf clubs.

Today, the Club, its owners and members, move on confidently towards a new century. By golfing standards in Britain, the club is a 'baby'. It will not celebrate its centenary until 2024 but much more has been crammed into Wentworth's 70 years than has happened in twice that time at other clubs around the country.

Setting the Scene

PETER DOBEREINER

Geology has a lot to answer for. Geology turned the Welsh into a nation of singers because in the remote mountain communities they had to make their own entertainment. Geology shaped the character of the Yorkshireman, God help it, just as it softened the speech and the nature of the people of the fertile plains. The particular geological characteristic which interests the golfer is, of course, sand because sand is quite literally the base for the finest golf courses.

Nowhere is the golfing virtue of sand seen to better advantage than on the area known as the Surrey Heath. This was once a vast forest and a royal hunting reserve but the advance of civilization displaced the wild boars and replaced them with the milder bores

known as golfers. This land is perfect for golf and when the game burst like a puffball in the late nineteenth century and spread its spores on the wind all over the world the Surrey heathland proved to be a receptive seedbed. Thanks to geology, these clubs became the aristocracy of inland golf, all of them sharing a common heritage of silver birch and pine, bracken and heather, and fine fescue turf.

This Surrey Heath also supported among its fauna a species of human being every bit as distinctive as its flora. As a professional golf-watcher, I have had to make frequent forays into the Surrey heathland and on first acquaintance with the area I was fascinated to observe the golf spectators. Thirty years ago there were no milling throngs for events like the Worplesdon Foursomes, just a handful of individual specimens of Surrey Man.

By this time, in the 1950s and 1960s, we were well into the third generation of this new hybrid breed, descendants of the original bright young things who habitually roared off down the Dover road in the highest of spirits, cloche hats and Bentley tourers for a weekend's 'goff' at Le Touquet where they were observed with wry amusement by P G Wodehouse and immortalized in his fiction. By the time I discovered Surrey Man the badges of tribal identity had become standardized as strictly as school uniforms.

The female of the species wore a twin set in pastel or autumnal shades, pearls, tweed skirt, sensible brogues, and her golden tresses were constrained beneath a Jacqmar scarf. These gorgeous visions, spiritual sisters of John Betjeman's Joan Hunter Dunn, were almost invariably orbited by prancing red setters or, on one memorable occasion, a half-couple of foxhounds.

The young men also favoured tweed, in the form of hacking jackets, worn in conjunction with canary-coloured waistcoats, cavalry twill trousers, cravats and tweed rat-catcher's caps pulled well down

The scent of the conifers, sound of
the bath,
The view from my bedroom of
moss-dappled path,
As I struggle with double-end
evening tie,
For we dance at the Golf Club,
my victor and I.

The Hillman is waiting, the light's
in the hall,
The pictures of Egypt are bright
on the wall,
My sweet, I am standing beside
the oak stair
And there on the landing's the
light on your hair.

By roads 'not adopted' by
woodlanded ways,
She drove to the club in the late
summer haze,
Into nine-o'clock Camberley,
heavy with bells
And mushroomy, pine-woody,
evergreen smells.

from
A Subaltern's Love-song
by John Betjeman

over the eyes. They conversed by means of a high-pitched braying sound which could be heard across three fairways.

Little did I realise that they were an endangered species, soon to be wiped out in the 'Big Bang' and the carnage of Lloyds names. Although isolated pockets of Surrey man could be found as far out as Woking, the main concentration of the breed was undoubtedly at Wentworth. The Wentworth estate was entirely populated by them and, indeed, the estate had been created between the wars specifically as a sanctuary for Surrey Man.

There were those who claimed they could identify subdivisions within the tribe, insisting that the Sunningdale version was quite distinct from the mainstream Wentworth populace. I could never see it, myself, although I did hear an ugly rumour that one Wentworth resident was 'in trade'. And I knew for a fact that two Wentworth club members were in show business – legitimate of course.

Those gilded creatures, Surrey Man and Surrey Woman, formed the human backdrop to the historical golfing events which created the reputation of the Wentworth courses.

I was not around for the occasion when the Walker Cup team put up a bit of black over the West course. Fred Corcoran, the American entrepreneur who had pioneered the men's professional golf tour in the United States, was engaged to create a tour for US women professionals. In order to generate publicity for the enterprise he brought a group of the first women pros over to Britain and challenged the Walker Cup team to a match. 'Mickers' – the inimitable Gerald Micklem whose influence on golf in this country was so significant, was slaughtered in his match and that reverse started an embarrassing rout.

Leonard – Leonard Crawley who was such an eccentric correspondent of *The Daily Telegraph* in later years – was so determined not to be outdriven by a woman that he hit a 1-iron off the first tee. His

Spectators at a tournament before the war

opponent, the redoubtable 'Babe' Zaharias, gave a wry smile, pulled the 1-iron out of her bag and smacked her tee shot twenty yards past Leonard's! The women won easily!

The Ryder Cup match of 1953 really put Wentworth on the map, with massive press coverage for days on end. The first sensation was when the Great Britain & Ireland Captain, Henry Cotton, banished his team's wives for the week. His reason was not the old boxing myth about a bit of how's-your-father weakening your legs but a desire to eliminate pillow talk critical of his selections and omissions and, therefore, damaging to team morale.

The United States won by a single point and the dung beetles of Fleet Street crucified the British youngsters Bernard Hunt and Peter Alliss, as if they had deliberately missed short putts at the end of their singles for perverse reasons of their own. It is, to coin a phrase, an ill wind that blows nobody any good. If the two crucial matches involving Alliss and Hunt had gone the other way, the American press would surely have destroyed Sam Snead who went completely to pieces in his single against Harry Weetman! As it was that *betise* passed unnoticed in the euphoria of America's victory.

The Club's name chosen by Golf Bag manufacturers Robert Bryant Ltd to add prestige to their most up-to-date model. Sixty years later Volvo named a car after the Club

(Right) The 1935 London Ladies' Foursomes at Wentworth. Dorritt Wilkins, represented Chigwell

Three years later, the Canada Cup put Wentworth into the spotlight of international attention. Ben Hogan liked to prepare himself as thoroughly as possible before he played important events. Accordingly, on the flight to Britain he asked his partner, Snead, to brief him on Wentworth's West course. Snead sat pondering for a long time over this enquiry, giving the impression that he was preparing a thorough analysis of every aspect of the course. At last he turned to Ben and replied laconically: 'It's a sonofabitch.' No matter. The United States won and Hogan took the individual honours with a total of 277.

My closest encounter with Surrey Woman was during the final of the first World Match-play tournament, between Arnold Palmer and Neil Coles. By this time, Surrey Man and Woman were a disappearing breed, fast being engulfed by the tidal wave of social change involving Beatlemania, the permissive society and the new barbarism.

On the twelfth hole Palmer pulled his drive into the woods. I hurried to where his ball lay in order to get a close-up view of the great man in his natural habitat. Into the woods he strode, frowning slightly because he always like to make the situation appear really desperate before he pulled off one of his miracle recoveries. The semicircle of

Joyce Wethered, playing for Worplesdon, watched by Pam Barton in the London Ladies' Foursomes

spectators behind his ball fell into respectful silence as Palmer set himself for the shot. At this moment, Surrey Woman insinuated herself between our frozen ranks and stopped right in front of me. She stooped, passing her shooting stick around behind her, placing its point on the toe of my right shoe and then settled her full weight on the seat.

She was a woman of a certain age and with a figure which we old Berkshire boys would describe as being bred more for pork than bacon. I clenched my teeth. Tears sprouted from my eyes. The reflex yelp of pain was stifled in my throat. Even Palmer himself would not have held me to blame if I had shouted out and ruined his shot – not once he had understood the reason for my outburst! But no sound issued from my lips, so I suppose I won that title for Palmer. I haven't missed a Match-play Championship at Wentworth from that day to this. Between whiles, I have played the Wentworth courses many times and have never tired of their magic.

Things change, as they must because we live in a changing world. Even the golf courses change because they are living entities and subtle alterations have to be made to them from time to time in order to keep them the way they were and were meant to be. The real point about Wentworth, however, is this: the courses transcend their narrow legal status of private property because they have become national treasures. In that sense, ownership involves the privilege of trustee-ship, a solemn duty to nourish and pass on the courses to new generations and the new tribes of the Surrey Heath.

Personalities

JOHN INGHAM

Years ago, in the days when British golfers wore army surplus and caddies slept among rhododendron bushes comedian Bob Hope arrived at Wentworth worried about a slice and anxious to find a sharp-eyed enthusiast able to carry six clubs, said by crooner Bing Crosby to be hickory shafted.

'Are you good at finding balls?' Hope asked one Wentworth caddie.

'Sure, there's none better.'

'Great. Then find one now, and we'll start,' said Bob, whose golf was far from comic.

When I first arrived at Wentworth for the 1953 Ryder Cup, they were still recalling this chestnut and the other one about tweedy golf writer Leonard Crawley whom we have read suffered the worst moment of his illustrious career in the USA lady professionals versus British amateurs match which found him facing the mighty 'Babe' Zaharias.

A fine cricketer and a Walker Cup competitor, Leonard played in striped shirts from Harvie and Hudson, an MCC tie, plus fours and polished brown brogues. As 'Babe' strode on to the tiger tee, Leonard apparently twitched his moustache and pointed a finger up the fairway towards the ladies' tee.

'No Len,' cracked the Babe. 'The back tees will suit me just fine!'

'Babe' Zaharias established three records in the 1932 Olympics, then turned to golf and won a string of tournaments before being voted the Greatest Female Athlete of the Half-Century. She went on to become the first women ever to be a head professional at any club! And when she set about Crawley she not only out hit him from the tee but overwhelmed him. The American ladies humiliated the whole team which, said one unkind soul, played so like rabbits that their noses twitched over the lunchtime salad.

And when we got to that 1953 Ryder Cup clash, nonplaying British Captain Henry Cotton said his squad of red-blooded athletes needed steak and physical training each morning which Harry Bradshaw and Fred Daly said was a piece of nonsense. The newspapers seized on the conflict and one evening edition displayed placards in the Wentworth driveway, mischievously informing the public 'Cotton lashes team softies'.

This was the match where Harry Weetman, a savage hitter, crashed five down against Sam Snead but then watched in amazement as the American's game literally fell apart with a series of wild hooks. Weetman, who liked to wear new, crocodile shoes, sensed the game was not up, took his chances and snatched an unexpected one hole victory. Suddenly this put ghastly pressure on two youngsters behind them who realized that Great Britain & Ireland could, in fact, win!

Sadly, Peter Alliss, fresh from National Service, and fair-haired Bernard Hunt, let the opportunity pass. Years later, the last green collapse by Alliss still haunted him. 'Everyone in golf saw me muff that greenside shot and everyone in golf told me my father would never have been so unprofessional,' said Peter. He made amends so marvel-lously in later Cup encounters that both Arnold Palmer and Dave Marr said they were glad Alliss did not compete regularly on the United States tour.

Peter Roscow, Secretary in 1953, ran the Ryder Cup in army style

Anyway, the Americans just scraped a victory by a single point in that encounter although the big winner of the week was undoubtedly the host club which proved, yet again, what an ideal venue Wentworth is for an international. Everything Wentworth does it does in style. So much so, in fact, that John Jay Hopkins brought his Canada Cup (now the World Cup) to Wentworth in 1956 with the most respected man in golf – Ben Hogan.

Once again, it was my privilege to be there. The excitement was electric as Hogan walked on to the first tee, Captain of possibly the all-time dream team of Hogan and Snead. As a young journalist, I had been too shy to attempt a pre-match interview with either player. I made do with the atmosphere and the sheer thrill of seeing our game complemented with such majestic skill. Besides, Ken Bousfield and Weetman told me the inside stories of the week! I discovered how Hogan had instructed Snead on the art of hitting better drives. 'All you have to do,' said Mr Hogan, 'is point your left toe a bit towards the target at the address . . . ' Of course, the Americans won. To them it was just another tournament. To us it was another huge bonus for Wentworth.

Television was beginning to flex its muscles in Britain at this time. The medium was to change sport totally, just as Cleveland lawyer Mark McCormack was to change our great game into a sports industry.

During the lull in 1961 as McCormack took over golf in the United Kingdom, I again talked my way into the English Amateur Championship staged that year at delightful Wentworth. The new Club administration had rightly decided that three golf writers – including myself – should be made honorary members (today all members of the Association of Golf Writers enjoy honorary status). Peter Roscow posted this item of news on the Board. It meant free practice rounds at no charge although in those days, as the *Golfer's Handbook* of the year indicates, the green fee was just £1!

Round one opponent Jack Chance either had a leg missing or had been in a serious accident. Either way, Scottish starter Hugh Docherty gave us the briefest of mentions and we were off. Mr Chance lost. Round Two was another story, however. Francis Fisher could hit the ball a country mile and so I made my excuses to Dai Rees's caddie, Little Mac, who wintered as a rule behind bars at Wandsworth thanks to a clever yet simple trick: he threw a brick through a shop window! This led the judge to order him inside, care of Her Majesty, for several of those chilly weeks when no one who could afford a caddie wanted to play. His ingenious ploy only came to light when *Daily Mail* golf writer Michael McDonnell was asked to give a lecture 'inside' to those poor folk who had fallen on hard times and spotted Little Mac in the captive audience.

Pat Vigers

NO ORDINARY MEMBER

After almost 70 years as a member, Wentworth's first lady recalls war, drama and, she confides, some 'frightful' happenings which can only now be decently exposed to public gaze.

As the old hunting lodge was blossoming into the modern clubhouse of today, Pat Vigers, born in 1899, remembers the day the Duke of Windsor and his unwanted guest were refused lunch; the 'wildly Irish' member who manhandled a nude female statue from its stand in the garden to perform a Fellini-style dance; and that awful moment, from the Club point of view, when she tried to propose a butcher as member.

All this in the days when champagne and cocktails were served in a clubhouse filled with potted plants, drunk to the quiet tinkling on the keyboard of the club's pianist, following a genteel round with wooden shafts on a course that seemed to have more trees and more graceful swans on the lake than now! Thankfully, the lake is being brought back to its former glory.

Pat Vigers remembers it all. She is a founder member and President of the Ladies' Section of the Wentworth Club. When she joined in 1926 she paid just £7 a year for the privilege but she chose to pay an extra £100 for a major share in a club destined to become known throughout the golfing world.

In those old Edwardian days the Duke of Windsor, a keep-fit enthusiast, would run down from his home at Fort Belvedere to the course, behind his chauffeur-driven motor – too dangerous to attempt today on Surrey's clogged roads! 'He said it reduced wind resistance to stay behind the car,' said Pat, born in the last October of the old century. 'He always did it. He was very fit.'

The Duke, she recalls, was involved in that 'shocking business' with Archie Compston, a giant-sized professional who was acclaimed by the public for beating Walter Hagen in the first unofficial Ryder Cup, but condemned by others because he swore like a trooper. The Duke, however, liked him and they played together many times. On one fateful occasion the Duke attempted to bring his guest Mr Compston into the clubhouse for lunch at Wentworth but they were halted in their tracks by the mighty Mrs Ena Williams who ran Wentworth's catering for years with an efficient Sandhurst-style discipline which made her respected but feared. There was a confrontation – similar to incidents at several other clubs.

The matter, it appeared, was not open for discussion. Even though Mr Compston was a good friend of the Duke, professional golfers, it was pointed out by

Bright-eyed Mac ended his days selling toy dogs that leapt and danced by means of squeezed air, on Oxford Street. He did rather better than Max Faulkner's Wentworth caddie. He was arrested in Piccadilly with a 5-iron and a ball, claiming he needed a 4 to win the Open!

I remember, too, going to Wentworth without clubs because I had discovered General Dwight D Eisenhower was to be allowed to play using one of those new fangled ride-on buggies. I saw the motorcade parked and the FBI guys in the bushes, frightfully conspicuous in their woeful attempts to be inconspicuous, and knew that the General would soon trundle down the last fairway of the West course which, in those days, was called the Burma Road because, I was told, it was as tough to play, as prisoners of war had found the real Burma Road to build. Ike, who later became President, and his playing partner, hero Arnold Palmer, were delighted to talk golf with a young scribe. Ike said his favourite shot was the 5-wood because it was so forgiving. I recall thinking that you could meet almost anyone in the

Mrs Williams, were not allowed in the dining room. The Duke, unused to being told what he could not do by the hired help, decided to lunch elsewhere without delay!

'Of course, times are different today,' says Mrs Vigers who learned golf with wooden shafted implements and bought a putter from former Club Professional 'dear Johnnie Aitken', and used no other throughout her career! Mind you, she admits that there have been wonderful improvements in the game today, although certain players in ghastly uncoordinated colours which shriek, leave much to be desired.

Pat Vigers, Ladies' Captain seven times, played in a skirt, spoke up for youngsters learning the game and never has tolerated what she calls snob attitudes.

When her husband was away on business abroad, she chose to open a gift shop in Sunningdale. Shocked Wentworth members told her she could not possibly go into what they called trade, but if she must, she should at least call the shop a boutique.

'It all got so difficult when the local butcher told me he would love to join the Club. I saw no reason why not but the Club would not hear of it.'

Even though Pat pointed out that they already had one member who sold a famous brand of rainwear in his West End shop, it made no difference. 'My butcher never got to join Wentworth . . .'

Pat Vigers (left) and Irene Corbin shake hands before the semi-final of the Daks Ladies' International Tournament at Wentworth in 1958, with Wanda Morgan in the background

Alf Sutton

PHYSIO TO THE STARS

English greengrocer, Alf Sutton, kicked by a horse and seriously injured in an extraordinary accident, slid into bankruptcy in 1952. Friends suggested he try for a new career – as attendant in Wentworth's locker room.

He landed the job and never looked back.

In order to 'get ahead' and earn enough to steer children through school, he decided to learn about physiotherapy. 'I had a great deal of support because there were many doctors here at Wentworth,' recalls Alf now a sprightly 75 years of age and already the recipient of a gold watch for services rendered.

So skilled did Alf become that many famous sportsmen went to him for treatment. Back in 1965 when the famous Australian Peter Thomson confronted a career threatening back problem, he was asked to attempt to get Thomson in a fit condition to compete in the World Match-play Championship.

'Thomson had fallen into a bunker and was in agony; he'd been told to quit golf for three months at least,' recalled Alf. 'When I first tried to help him, he cried out in agony. A Wentworth doctor had referred him to me and I had the job of trying to loosen him up.'

It all seemed hopeless but Thomson said he had only to reach the first tee to earn a guaranteed £3,000 and asked Alf please to try harder.

'I told him not to swing anything more than a wedge. This was on the Wednesday, with the tournament starting next day!' Newspaper cameramen took Alf's picture, trying to rescue Thomson's career. For Alf it was all thrilling stuff.

Amazingly, Thomson won his opening match in extra holes and went on to the final, where he lost to Gary Player, but only by 3 and 2 in the two round final. Much of the credit that week should have gone to Alf, who rescued the damaged muscle!

Alf had proved himself! Now a fully qualified performer, he was obliged to be covered by what they call the Doctors Defence, an insurance for £1 million which gives cover in case something untoward happens during treatment.

Something soon turned up. It was way past midnight when the phone rang in Alf's home. On the line was someone representing Jack Nicklaus. 'Can you do us a favour?' was the question, and I reckon it was

Jack's then manager, Mark McCormack, on the line. Apparently, Jack had pinched a nerve playing tennis. Could I help? They sent Jack round in a car for treatment and I remember it was a Rolls Royce and that there were bottles of wine everywhere!'

Alf in his pyjamas, had to give Nicklaus some traction and it all worked out quite well – Jack was on the first tee next day and was not suffering any pain! Alf had 'done the business'.

'You have to take care because there are one or two cowboys about but the real expert can free a joint in two minutes. Always beware the man who suggests you book a series of appointments! The lower back is where it's at, and you have to take care,' says Alf who carried his own clubs well into his mid-seventies, still smokes a cigar whenever possible, and who admits he landed on his feet at Wentworth.

'I always remember what Arnold Palmer told me. He said it does not matter what the swing looks like, as long as it repeats.'

Alf Sutton was thinking of that the day he holed in one at the tenth! Great days, great times for the man who never has regretted being kicked by a horse!

world at Wentworth, and if you knew how to behave, you could have a splendid time. Sadly for me, the story arrived too late for the paper to print it, and it was cruelly spiked!

Of all the moments I recall, I would have to go to the fourth green in the inaugural World Match-play Championship final where Neil Coles and his caddie 'Chingy' had Palmer three down for my best memory. Coles needed two putts to go four up which would surely clinch matters, but he three-putted. Enraged, he hit his foot with the putter. 'I hit it really hard,' Neil was to tell me later, 'and was in pure agony. What could I do in front of those people – scream in pain?'

Winnie Wooldridge

DETERMINED COMPETITOR

Winnie Wooldridge was admired and loved by everyone because of her ability to play serious golf with a friendly attitude that never faltered. To Winnie, golf was a game to be enjoyed as much as she had enjoyed tennis during her years as one of Britain's top stars in that sport.

She reached the quarterfinals of Wimbledon twice and represented Britain in the Wightman Cup seven times – testimony to her skill as a player and her determination as a competitor. Win or lose, she always acted with grace and dignity.

When Winnie turned to golf at Wentworth she did not abandon tennis. She coached many youngsters and captained several junior sides but as golf took up

more and more of her time she worked hard at reducing her handicap to single figures and achieved a 'plus' rating.

She played for Surrey for the first time in 1978, retaining her place for the next twelve years. Pride in performance was her trademark. She earned a Scottish cap in 1982, won the Surrey Ladies' Championship in 1987 and again in 1990. That same year, she won the Wentworth Ladies' Open at what would turn out to be her last attempt.

Three times she was named Scottish Sportswoman of the Year, once when Bernard Gallacher was Scottish sportsman.

Those who were privileged to know her lost a very good friend when she died in 1992 at the tragically young age of only 44.

Winnie Wooldridge, who as Winnie Shaw, reached the quarter-finals at Wimbledon. Here at a pre-Wimbledon practice session she is chatting with Jenny Heron while Martina Navratilova (seated) looks on

Then Arnold Palmer scored three birdies in a row and Neil Coles, the best English golfer in the world in those days, failed to bring off the miracle win.

So what is it that makes Wentworth special and why do we feel such a sense of expectancy as we turn into the leafy drive, in my case, driving into what I call the rear entrance? It has to be pedigree. For starters, go back to the 1920s when Sir Ernest Holderness just lost the Surrey title to Major Thornburn, then recall that the Curtis Cup began here in 1932, and that Archie Compston, Club Professional at Wentworth, won the Surrey Open at Wentworth in 1947. Remember too, that the world's greatest players have been delighted to walk these

Mindy Blake

SUPER ENTHUSIAST

Mindy Blake DSO, DFC, MSC did not take up golf until he was 34 but he became one of the game's keenest students of technique and wrote a hugely successful book on the subject. When he retired from the RAF in 1958 to become an engineering consultant, he turned

his attention to inventing a golf trainer called the Swingrite which was so well received that he manufactured and sold it worldwide.

Inventing things was nothing new to Mindy, a slightly built man who came to England from New Zealand to join the RAF and 'satisfy his thirst for adventure'.

David De Ville, writing in the Wentworth Club magazine in 1985, recalled that Mindy survived three flying accidents, two of them intentional! He deliberately ditched a Spitfire in August 1941 to test his survival theory and successfully devised a way to prevent pilots killing themselves when ditching. The following year, injured and about to crash, he deliberately put his plane into a near vertical dive having first opened the cockpit canopy and loosened his seat straps. He had deduced that the speed with which he was heading for the water would suck him out of the cockpit in a parabolic arc high enough for him to use his parachute. Fortunately, his theory was proved correct and his parachute opened before he hit the sea. He survived only to be picked up by a German launch and spent the rest of the war in Stalag Luft III. He tried but failed to escape.

Hostilities over, Blake's tremendous devotion to the game was such that, incredibly, his name appears on nine of the Club's thirteen competition winner boards. He won four of the competitions more than once and his total tally was fourteen!

Today, his memory is honoured and perpetuated by the Mindy Blake Memorial Trophies purchased by donation from members three years after his untimely death in 1981 following a second heart attack.

fairways – Hogan, Cotton, Snead, Tony Lema, Gary Player, Bobby Locke, Peter Thomson, Jack Nicklaus and more recently Nick Faldo, Sandy Lyle, Seve Ballesteros. The list is endless. Wentworth is not a Surrey club nor an English club. It is one of the most significant of world clubs and, as such, it has a duty to maintain a very high standard indeed and does.

Sensibly, the Club has spared no expense where it matters – out on the golf courses. When I was a youngster, the third green on the West could make you feel very foolish. Even Lloyd Mangrum of the United States putted short up the old slope and watched his ball roll back right off the green from where he had to chip. It was, to be blunt,

Ena Williams
SIXTY YEARS OF LOYALTY

One of the Wentworth Club's most notable characters, whose reign extended across six decades, was Ena Williams who managed the bar and the dining room. During the war when the clubhouse was taken over by the army, Mrs Williams was responsible, under the Club Secretary Major Rawlinson (known to everybody as Rawly) for safeguarding the Club's wines and spirits in the bushes, of all places, before establishing a temporary clubhouse in the changing huts at the swimming pool and subsequently at Kingsbourn and the Dormy House.

Ena Williams, christened Thomasena but always know as Ena, was born and bred in Northumberland. The eldest of a family of twelve children, she came down to Surrey at the age of 21 and was recruited to the staff of Wentworth club in 1930. Throughout her life she retained her northern qualities. She was outspoken, straightforward, hard working and loyal. As many Club members could testify, she did not suffer fools gladly. The rules of the Club were there to be observed by members and visitors, grown ups as well as children. There were no exceptions; not even royalty. Even before she became Manageress she informed the then Prince of Wales that there was a fee for playing a round of golf at Wentworth 'and if you don't pay you don't play'. The Prince's companion solved the problem by pointing out that the Prince was, in fact, playing with the Club Professional, Archie Compston!

In an era when conformity to dress regulations

was far stricter than today's more easy going attitude, ensuring their observance was not always easy. But it was all in a day's work for Ena and, though many members and visitors may have been irritated at the time, they learned to recognize that Ena was scrupulously fair. Certainly her northern directness was tempered by an equal flow of kindness and affection. Over the years, during the many functions at the Club, Canada Cup, Ryder Cup, World Match-play tournaments and many others which were all demanding of her time, she was helpful to players, members of the press and visitors alike. She was an integral part of the Wentworth scene and a popular figure with everybody.

a trifle freakish. So the green was relaid more than once before everyone was happy it was fair.

Wentworth, too, has always placed great store on having a good professional to look after members. The late Tom Haliburton, who competed in the Ryder Cup, may have had something of a temper if assistants did not behave but he was always correctly described as a gentleman and gave his successor Bernard Gallacher, a fellow-Scot, a recommendation which has been proved sound over the years.

The Club, too, has enjoyed superb back-room boys and girls. Develop a twinge coming down the eighteenth and dear old Alf Sutton was always there to straighten you out in the physio room.

Wentworth has become 5-Star through sensible stewardship and has been helped by its continual association with the game's super-stars. In this regard, I hope to see a painting, displayed somewhere in the clubhouse, of Ben Hogan, the quiet competitor who lit the golf taper which was later fanned so brilliantly by Palmer, Nicklaus and Player. Hogan, you see, simply had to walk to the practice tee in that

Dick Powell

FROM ONE OLD SOLDIER TO ANOTHER!

Old Eighth Army soldier Dick Powell was given three weeks notice that Allied Supreme Commander, General Eisenhower, wished to play the West course and might like an American-style electric or petrol driven cart.

As Caddiemaster, Dick was not best pleased. There would be no job for a caddie and, in those post war days, battery-driven buggies were thin on the ground in England anyway!

Somehow Dick managed to borrow one and spent several days hard work with polish, sprucing up the vehicle for the General.

When Powell was introduced to the General, his every move was watched by American security. 'We have your buggy ready,' said Dick. 'Thank you, soldier,' retorted Ike, 'but I prefer to walk . . .'

'Well make your bloody mind up!' snapped back Dick, revealing years later that after all his effort, and with the tension of meeting the big man, he somehow lost his wits.

'It was all right; he understood and gave me a twenty dollar bill. I'll never forget it with all those security people around.'

Dick Powell was appointed temporary Caddiemaster in 1949 and retains the title even today. When he started there were 50 caddies but these days the number has dwindled. 'Caddies are dying out; they charge too much at £25 a round.'

Dick caddied at Wentworth in 1932 when they staged the Curtis Cup matches there. He drew an American and they had to play the famous Diane Fishwick, wife of Brigadier-General Alfred Cecil Critchley CMG, CBE, DSO *who was himself a Wentworth stalwart. Mrs Fishwick won, but the Americans collected the trophy.*

Years later, Dick was charged with running the caddies for the Canada Cup which saw Ben Hogan and Sam Snead score a memorable victory. 'I had to assemble more than 90 caddies for that, and I always remember General Critchley admitting the it would be a tough job. He just said, "Good luck . . ." '

Dick carried clubs, too, for Lord Brabazon but blundered badly! 'At the first hole he gave me an apple and two biscuits. I thanked him and ate the apple first, then the biscuits because I'd had no breakfast. At the tenth he asked for the apple. I said I'd eaten it. Then he said he wanted the biscuits for his dog. I said I'd eaten them, too! He didn't like it!'

rather ordinary, buttoned-up, grey cardigan to attract a gathering of other tournament players. They wanted to learn. Nobody spoke as caddie Cecil Timms handed over an iron. You noticed that Hogan did not wear a left-hand glove, dressed in subdued colours of grey topped by a proper, white, golfing cap and that his trousers were surprisingly turned up in case he had to play from long, damp grass.

I recall Hogan opening one round with a 3 in that 1956 Canada Cup when he chipped into the hole from just off the green. Then he scored a 2 and people started running up the third fairway, uncontrolled by stewards carrying long bamboo sticks! Hogan could be ruffled as he showed at the eleventh where, just as he was about to start his backswing, a dog raced across the tee. Hogan backed off and went through his pre-drive routine again. Then the Great Man hooked it into silver birch trees. There was a crack but the ball broke to the right and came into view again as we all felt it must and should.

Just watching Hogan will live forever in my mind. As Bob Hope would say: 'Wentworth – thanks for the memory!'

Bert Collyer,
Assistant Caddiemaster

And when Dick carried the Duke of Windsor's clubs, the Duke asked him what he should call him. 'I told him Dick and asked him what I should call him. "That's a good question," said the Duke. Then he said that since his name was David, which surprised me

because I thought it was Edward, I should call him that!

'Out on the course he asked me, "Dick, do you smoke?" And I said, "Yes, thanks very much," and he said, "No, I am not offering you one! I want a cigarette and did not bring mine with me!" I gave him one of my three Woodbines and he thanked me!' At the end of the game he gave Dick five shillings, a lot of money in those days. Dick recalls, ' He asked what I'm going to do with it. I said the boys will have a drink down at the local pub, and he asks its name. I get there and there are seven of us caddies and we play some darts when in walks the Duke and sits right next to me and asks to join in the game as my partner. What a moment for me but the lads had the last laugh! The Duke and I lost and we had to buy drinks all round!'

Dick can also remember being offered £1,000 by a member, if he could help the man break 80 on the West course. At the last, Dick had been so helpful the man could take 9 and still break 80! Financially pressed, the member suddenly wanted to try out a new swing! He sent several teeshots flying into the great unknown. It wasn't cricket.

'I had some great times and I'll tell you what,' says Dick, 'It won't ever be the same.'

But then, what is?

The Professionals

RAYMOND JACOBS

By any standards, the roll call of the six professionals who have served at Wentworth makes impressive reading. Five of them played on Ryder Cup teams – George Duncan, who was attached to the club from 1924 to 1929, Archie Compston (1945-1949), Jimmy Adams (1949-1952), Tom Haliburton (1952-1975) and his successor the present incumbent – Bernard Gallacher. The exception was John Aitken (1929-1945), but he had one virtue in common with Duncan, Adams, Haliburton and

George Duncan, the Club's first professional, regularly made the front cover of the golfing magazines

ABE MITCHELL (St. Albans) (Left) and GEORGE DUNCAN (Wentworth)
starting out in the final of the Professional Tournament at Roehampton.

FOLLOWING IN FATHER'S FOOTSTEPS.
George Duncan, it seems, believes in "catching them young." He is here seen giving a few "tips" to his eight-years-old son—another George, by the way—who, despite his tender years, is already making good progress in his efforts to master the intricacies of the Royal and Ancient Game.

Gallacher – he was Scottish-born, one more in the long line of expatriate professionals who clambered over Hadrian's Wall in the confident expectation that the grass, certainly at Virginia Water, would be a good deal greener than it was at home.

Although they form a tiny minority, there are still clubs in Scotland of the first rank which still do not employ a professional. That was never the policy at Wentworth which from the start set its cap at the upper echelons of the game. The terms of employment then, not to mention the language in which they were couched, were very different from today, and even after relative values, inflation and the rest have been taken into account, the retainers offered in the 1920s look feudally meagre.

When Duncan was appointed the Club's first professional he had won the Open Championship four years before, yet his basic salary was £100 a year – at the prices then prevailing the equivalent of, say, four thousand measures of whisky.

Duncan, one of ten children born to the wife of an Aberdeenshire village policemen, was initially a carpenter but had turned to professional golf by the time he was seventeen. He arrived at Wentworth via club jobs in Scotland and North Wales and at the old Hanger Hill club in Ealing. A player of brilliance and inspiration, he won the 1920 Open, having been thirteen strokes behind the leader Abe Mitchell after two rounds. At its best Duncan's game was 'the champagne of golf and the fizziest champagne at that'. James Braid once wrote of him: 'He plays so fast he looks as if he doesn't care.' It came as no surprise when Duncan's autobiography was called *Golf at the Gallop*.

Apart from the Open, 'miss 'em quick' Duncan had a number of considerable achievements to his name, not least in man-to-man combat. He beat Braid for the 1913 British Professional Match-play title and Jock Hutchison and Walter Hagen in the two unofficial matches between Britain and the United States which preceded the Ryder Cup. In the first two Cup encounters Duncan beat Joe Turnesa, one of six brothers who turned professional, and in 1929 he beat Hagen, his opposite number as Captain, by the sumptuous margin of 10 and 8.

Yet Duncan had by then resigned from Wentworth 'to become a freelance to play exhibitions and challenge matches'. Four years later, however, perhaps attracted to the security in the uncertain economic times of that period of a more stable existence, Duncan joined the Mere club, in Cheshire, where he stayed for the rest of his working life.

By coincidence, Duncan's successor, Aitken, also spent time at the Hanger Hill club before he began his sixteen year career at Wentworth in April 1929. More celebrated as a club maker than as a player, Aitken brought Norman Sutton with him as his assistant. The terms of his first contract are worth scrutinizing. The Club's Board took over the shop having purchased all Duncan's stock. Aitken was paid just over £4 a week and took a third of the profits from 'items sold,

Johnnie Aitken, one of five Scots to have held the post of Club Professional

repairs and tuition plus an optional bonus based on the success he made of the job'. In the early years of the Second World War Aitken's salary was unchanged but his profit share was increased to a half and when he retired in 1945 Aitken received a £50 handshake.

Some things, however, do not change. In 1930 Aitken's shop was broken into twice. The first time £30 worth of stock was taken. In the second incident the safe was stolen!

Compston was hardly at Wentworth long enough to experience such misfortunes. A contemporary of Duncan, he, too, played in the first three Ryder Cup matches and also had one notable competitive disaster and one remarkable triumph. In the 1930 Open Championship, Compston took the lead with a record breaking third round of 68 at Hoylake, only to suffer the greatest disappointment by taking 82 in the final round to finish equal sixth, six strokes behind Bobby Jones on his march to the Grand Slam. Two years before, however, in a 72 hole challenge match at Moor Park, Compston had beaten Walter

commencement of the club's return journey. The left heel is quickly returning to its original position, and the left shoulder is acting as a powerful lever, resulting in a straightening of the left arm in No. 9. In Nos. 10, 11 and 12 the body has completely "unpivoted" from the hips, and the wrists are thrusting the club-head at great speed "through" the ball. It is this action of the wrists which makes the crispness of Duncan's shots such a delight to witness. In No. 13 the arms are going out after the ball, but the body is firmly "anchored" by the player's head to enable the body to complete its pivoting. The three concluding pictures show the completion of the follow-through, the weight of the body being very definitely supported by the left leg in No. 16.

A George Duncan swing sequence from
Golf Illustrated

(Left) Compston driving from the third at Wentworth

(Below) Archie Compston enjoying the sunshine in Bermuda

Jimmy Adams succeeded Archie Compston as the Club Professional

Hagen by 18 and 17, a drubbing from which the resilient American recovered almost at once to win his second Open at Sandwich.

Compston, born at Wolverhampton, had been paid a £100 annual retaining fee and when he resigned in 1948 – to redefine his uncompromising personality and volatile temper amid the balmy weather and tinkling sophistication of the Mid-Ocean Club in Bermuda – he was succeeded by Jimmy Adams whom the committee elevated to a £200 retainer. Adams, who took up the professional's post in January of the following year, was born in Troon. He had a long and lissome swing, remarkable for one of his somewhat ample build and girth. Indeed, it was only possible to swing the way he did because he was double-jointed. An equally smooth putting stroke enabled him to finish runner-up twice in the Open Championship before the Second World War and to play in the first four Ryder Cup teams to challenge the United States after hostilities had ended.

Yet Adams, unsettled in the job because he could not see a reliable future either at the club or in Britain, resigned in January 1952 to emigrate to Australia. He eventually returned and in 1979 was made an honorary member but on his departure Adams was immediately replaced by Tom Haliburton, who presided until his untimely death 23 years later. Born at Rhu in Dunbartonshire in the west of Scotland, Haliburton was a professional typical of his generation in that he combined his duties at the club with successful tournament play – a diversity of interest which Haliburton's successor, Bernard Gallacher, was able to fulfil as well. By then, however, such division of

Tom Haliburton

A GOLFING GENTLEMAN

Of all his many qualities, it was as a teacher and a communicator that Tom Haliburton will be remembered longest by those privileged to have known him well. It was with the young, however, that he had a special gift. No junior golfer could be more fortunate than to have spent his formative years under Tom's watchful eye.

Like some before and many after him, he knew the essential mechanics of the golf swing inside out and could demonstrate them endlessly with that full rounded swing of his, a swing that went so well with his genial character and gentle demeanour. Even more important was his huge understanding of how golf worked, what it took to get that irritating little pellet round eighteen holes in the least number of shots.

Only when I grew older did I realize how rare was his great understanding of the game and even rarer his ability to impart it to others.

Yet Tom was far more than just a great teacher. Quite simply, he was a beautiful player, as neat and tidy in his golf as he was in his demeanour and attire. Never a careless shot, never a hurried, thoughtless stroke and with a little touch of the white cap, there he was with a score in the mid 60s without ever seeming to have played quite that well.

Like so many of his generation, the war probably took away his best years. A string of victories in 1938 in his native Scotland indicated that he was just learning the art of turning sweet play into meaningful reward. But then it was off to the RAF for seven years. Afterwards, he never seemed quite able to do full justice to his talent in competition.

Often there were spectacular cameo roles, never more so than when he set a world record of 126 for 36 holes at Worthing in 1952. However, a seven shot lead at halfway was still not enough to ensure victory the following day.

Perhaps it was this highly visible failure, rather than the spectacular play that preceded it, that stayed in the minds of the selectors when it came to choosing the team for the following year's Ryder Cup matches at Wentworth. Only a year into his position as Club Professional there, failure to make the team on his home course was a bitter disappointment.

Ryder Cup honours did come in 1961 and 1963

The perfect Club Professional

but by then he was in his mid 40s and with the likes of Palmer, Casper and Lema rampant on the world scene, there were not many points for British players to win.

Tom came pretty close to being the perfect club pro. As well as his great teaching skills, he put together one of the best professional shops in the country, was a delight to play with and developed a string of good young assistants, many of whom went on to golfing honours and good club jobs. An apprenticeship under Tom Haliburton was as good a grounding as you could have.

One of my own last memories of Tom is of a game on the West course one summer's afternoon. Already slowing perceptibly, he needed a 3-wood to reach the green at the par 3 fourteenth, bouncing the ball into the face of the bank in front of the green and up on to the putting surface. I still remember an acute sense of futility at hitting a 6-iron to 10 feet and two-putting to lose the hole. Tom took only 23 putts that afternoon and was round in 65; the perfect example not of how, but of how many.

BRUCE CRITCHLEY

forces was becoming increasingly rare among professionals plumping either for the security of a club job or trying their hands as tournament players on the embryo PGA European Tour.

Haliburton graduated to Wentworth through several clubs north and south of the border and had been chief assistant to Henry Cotton at Temple just before the Second World War. He had numerous tournament successes, played in two Ryder Cup sides and he was elected Captain of the Professional Golfers' Association in 1969. He was well known for his habitual courtesy which hid a temper notorious for its short fuse when a shot displeased him. His firmly controlled swing and a putting stroke, distinctive for the rap it gave the ball, took Haliburton to many notable competitive achievements. His most celebrated performance left him holder of the lowest tournament score on the British circuit for many years, 61 in the 1952 Spalding tournament at Worthing, to which he added 65 to hold the world record of 126 for successive rounds. Few have since beaten either mark.

Although the fact and the circumstances could not have been foreseen then, Haliburton established for the Club its professional line of succession in 1969 when he met Bernard Gallacher playing in his first Ryder Cup match at Royal Birkdale at Southport. It was the first of the eight in which Gallacher would play before he became the team's captain, as Eric Brown, also born in Bathgate, West Lothian, had once been. A distinguished amateur career behind him, Gallacher turned professional at eighteen, was Rookie of the Year in 1968 and in 1969 firmly established himself with his first two tournament victories and three second place finishes to lead the Order of Merit with £6,793, a sum which·in 1992 barely earned a spot in the top 200, on the Volvo Tour. Gallacher was attached to Ifield in Sussex when Haliburton asked the young Scot to move to Wentworth as a tournament assistant.

It may have been earlier than he would have liked to latch on to a club job but the shrewd Gallacher was not about to ignore the opportunity to join such a respected figure in the game at such a respected club. He and Guy Hunt, now a Volvo Tour tournament official, arrived at Wentworth in February 1970 and six years later Gallacher took over the job he has held ever since. The circumstances were, however, uniquely tragic. Having just started a practice round with Gallacher on the East course, Haliburton collapsed on the first green and died. Aged 60, he had been thinking of retiring and had recommended Gallacher to the Club as his successor. Gallacher duly took over in February 1975, believing the shorter circuit in those days with fewer tournaments made it feasible to play tournaments and also hold down a club professional's post. He was aware, too, of the occupational stability it offered to a young and growing family. The arrangement, unknown nowadays among leading tournament players, has proved mutually advantageous.

Bernard Gallacher

MOTIVATED BY PRIDE

Bernard Gallacher became Wentworth's Club Professional much earlier than planned when his predecessor, Tom Haliburton, died suddenly. Unknown to Gallacher, Haliburton had already singled out Gallacher as his successor when he moved to Wentworth as assistant from the Ifield club.

'Tom was a great man. I respected him so much. He taught me so much – not least, how to behave properly. He taught me discipline. He smoothed off the rough edges.'

Not many have been able to combine a tournament playing career with the duties of running a shop and giving lessons but the young Scot faced up to his new challenge off the course with the same determination he had shown in the Ryder Cup. His philosophy over the years has been simple enough. The extent of anyone's success is measured by the amount of hard work that person puts in.

Gallacher was not born with a silver spoon in his mouth. He played until he was fourteen with cut down second-hand clubs given to him by his father and uncles, and did not stay amateur long enough to aspire to Walker Cup status. He comes from Bathgate, halfway between Glasgow and Edinburgh in the industrial central belt of Scotland. He learned his golf on an eighteen hole course crammed into a pocket of land no self-respecting course architect would look at today. Yet, it was for Gallacher, and many of the other youngsters he grew up with, the focal point of the town. At Bathgate the lads played football in the winter and golf in the summer.

He found golf frustrating at first. Football, running and swimming were much easier to handle but Gallacher loves a challenge, and the physical effort of just trying to hit the ball properly was all he needed to whet his appetite.

Gallacher discovered, too, that he enjoyed competing and, as he grew stronger and began to hit the ball further, golf became his burning obsession. In local club Open events within a 35 mile radius of his home, he broke almost every course record and his 'winnings' as an amateur – paid by voucher, of course – enabled him to buy the equipment he might not otherwise have been able to afford.

Former Ryder Cup Captain – the late Eric Brown

who led the side that drew the 1969 match – had also been a Club member.

'I knew all about him but I never had any idols,' says Gallacher. 'I didn't copy Eric because I did not know him. Instead, I tried to emulate the best amateur players at the Club and later, when I turned professional, I would walk round and watch Christy O'Connor play. In 1968 when I turned pro he was the best player around and his course management was tremendous. So, too, was that of another of my Lothians golf colleagues – the late, lamented Ronnie Shade of Walker Cup and Eisenhower Trophy fame. What I learned was that when Christy and Ronnie missed the green they did not worry about it. They ambled down and chipped and putted for par as if that was the natural thing to do.'

He turned professional in 1967 and with few sponsors about in those days it was tough. In 1968 he scraped a living and at the start of 1969, with just £200 in his pocket he went out to southern Africa knowing that he had to make money to keep going. With two wins, a second and a third, he made enough to buy a sports car and make life on the 1969 British Tour more pleasant. He quickly reaped the rewards.

He won the second tournament he played in Britain, the Schweppes PGA Championship at Ashburnham, driving well and chipping and putting superbly. He was hardly ever out of the top three that spring and summer but could not qualify for the Ryder Cup team. In those days, players were selected according to their form over two seasons. Fortunately, team Captain, Brown, had six wild card selections and he gave one to Gallacher, the 1969 top earner.

'Being chosen was a great thrill and all I was disappointed about was not being chosen to play in all the series, but I have always accepted the captain's decision was final. On the last day another team member, Alex Caygill, and myself were not chosen for the first series of singles. Eric Brown told us one of us would play in the afternoon. I was pleased it was me . . . and I think Alex was too because my opponent was Lee Trevino whom I had beaten in an exhibition match in Scotland a couple of months earlier. I felt I had nothing to fear. I was playing well and the crowd inspired me. Some people have been put off by Lee Trevino's chat and comments between shots but I knew he was not trying to put me off and I felt comfortable. I beat him 4 and 3.

Gallacher's victory contributed to the fact that the match was drawn, with Jack Nicklaus conceding a last green putt to Tony Jacklin – an act of sportsmanship which highlighted the special qualities of the man and the game.

Gallacher's career as a Ryder Cup man – he would later captain the side – was off to a good start. From 1969 to 1983 he was ever present in the team, winning great matches against Lee Trevino in 1969 and later Jack Nicklaus.

'I managed to avoid Jack Nicklaus in Ryder Cup matches until 1977! It was a great moment for me to be drawn against him but it was marred by the fact that somehow, somewhere between the practice putting green and the first tee, my centre shafted putter disappeared. It never turned up. I had to go into the professional's shop and get another but in some ways it was a blessing in disguise. I had not been putting well with it and I did all right with the Ping blade I bought!

'I was jumpy on the tee but Jack always calms you down. He wants you to have a good game. He is super to play against. I felt at ease and what a start I made. Jack hit a 3-iron to the front edge. I was on the green. He chipped up to 5 feet and I putted down to 2 feet. Jack missed and then, to my astonishment, he gave me my putt! I was one up.

'He was bunkered left of the tee at the next two holes and I won both with par. When I birdied the fourth I cold hardly believe I was four up. I missed a chance to go five up and then he began gradually to chip away at my lead. When he holed a birdie putt across the green at the sixteenth we were all square.

'I knew the fans were saying that was that; it had been a good game and I had given Jack a good fight but Nicklaus was going to win. I had other ideas.

'At the seventeenth, I rolled in a putt of 85 feet – someone went out afterwards and measured it accurately – to go one up again and sank a five-footer on the last to win the point. Overall, the match was lost but winning that point was one of the proudest moments of my career.'

Winner of seventeen titles during his career, Gallacher never had the desire to travel to America and play the US Tour the way Jacklin and Oosterhuis did but he is proud of his French and Spanish Open victories scored after he became Club Professional at Wentworth. Gallacher, who coaches the Curtis Cup side, has served

on the European Tour committee for many years and is currently on the Tour's Board of Management putting much back into the game that he feels has been good for him. In recent years, his reputation has prompted his appointment to the government sponsored Sports Council and he is currently on the committee of the Duke of Edinburgh's hugely successful awards scheme. He and his attractive wife Leslie with children Kirsty (seventeen), Jamie (sixteen) and Laura Kate (six) live comfortably on the Wentworth Estate – a world apart from where it all began for him in Bathgate.

Hugely respected in the game, Gallacher has been, and will continue to be, a true ambassador for the Club. The Wentworth members were as proud as he was of his appointment to succeed Tony Jacklin as Ryder Cup Captain in 1991 – a fitting reward for a lifetime of service to the game, and he is still only 45!

RENTON LAIDLAW

The Courses

East and West

COLIN CALLANDER

The Wentworth Club has seen a good deal of change since it was established in 1924 but in one sense things have not changed at all. When Walter George Tarrant purchased the estate for a total of £42,000 from Ada Cabrera in 1920 he had a dream to build a club which would be seen as the model to which all other developers would aspire. Tarrant was not interested in compromises. He had his sights set on creating a masterpiece and it is to their great credit that successive owners of Wentworth have remained receptive to his aims.

Little documentary evidence of Tarrant's dream remains but what we do know is that one of the first decisions he made on

Harry Colt, (opposite) designer of classic courses, whose original ideas at Wentworth have stood the test of time

purchasing the beautiful acres site was to invite Harry Shapland Colt to design the original course. The two men had been involved with each other a decade earlier on a successful project at St George's Hill where Tarrant's first revolutionary vision of a prestigious golf club set in landscaped ground and surrounded by lavish homes had taken shape. Clearly, Tarrant had been impressed with the course at St George's Hill because it seems he did not wait for a second opinion before he brought the same architect to Wentworth. Nothing remains which tells us when the deal was done but we do know that the first eighteen holes – mostly now the holes forming the East course – at Wentworth were constructed and in play before the first meeting of the Club was called at 2.00pm on 1 November 1924.

Such business practice might well be abhorred in the 1990s but in the 1920s it seems that Tarrant's dictatorial tendencies did not cause the slightest stir and neither did his choice of course architect. In the 1920s, golf course architects did not enjoy the same high status that Robert Trent Jones and his contemporaries do in the 1990s but, that notwithstanding, Colt was still discussed in reverential tones in clubhouses throughout the British Isles. Seventy years on, Colt is regarded as the forefather of British golf course architecture, a tribute he richly deserves. During a working life which spanned the 50 years from the 1880s well into the 1930s, he designed or remodelled in excess of 100 courses in Britain and elsewhere. He was a master of his trade and is still regarded as such three decades after his death.

Colt was a qualified solicitor and a good enough golfer to win through to the last four of the Amateur Championship at Hoylake in 1906 and to represent England as an amateur in 1908. It was not his golf but his unique talent as a course designer, however, which brought him lasting fame.

During his career, Colt was responsible for creating some of Britain's finest courses. The list is impressive: Royal Portrush (1888), Rye (1894), Sunningdale Old (1901), Stoke Poges (1908), Swinley Forest (1909), Denham (1910), St George's Hill (1912), Camberley Heath (1913), Pyle and Kenfig (1922), Moor Park (1923) and Trevose (1924). In addition, he made major alterations at such prestigious clubs as Royal Porthcawl, Southerndown, Alwoodley, Aberdovey and Royal Dublin and lesser changes at Royal Lytham and St Annes, and Muirfield.

Colt's golfing options

Harry Colt believed that great holes should give the golfer an option.

He was not a great believer in compulsory carries from the tee but he did approve of using bunkers and other features to bring the best out of a golfer.

A good example of this was the sixteenth hole on his original course at Wentworth (now the sixteenth on the East course). Nowadays, standing on the tee, a golfer has to choose whether he wants to go for the carry over a row of bunkers which spreadeagle the fairway or deliberately come up short. In the 1920s, members and visitors were confronted with a rather different option.

When Colt designed the hole, the bunkers did not stretch all the way across the fairway as they do now but were positioned one behind each other slightly to the left of centre of the fairway. They presented a daunting threat but one which could be circumnavigated or avoided altogether.

The idea behind this design was to tempt the low handicapper to drive down the sliver of fairway on the left-hand side of the bunkers. It was not wide but if the drive was accurate enough it would avoid the sand and rough and would set up a relatively straightforward shot to the green.

Colt believed that good golfers would choose this option but he also realized that it would not be fair to force the high handicapper to do the same.

With this in mind, he left a wide open space to the right of the sand into which the high handicappers could hit their tee shots. This meant that the golfer was giving up his chance of getting up to the green in two shots but it did afford a safer option.

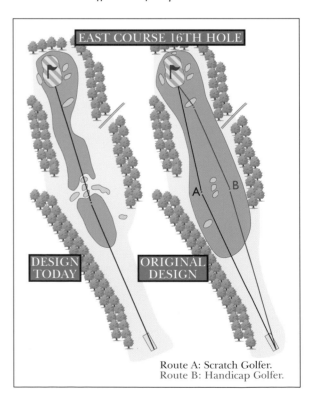

EAST COURSE 16TH HOLE

DESIGN TODAY

ORIGINAL DESIGN

Route A: Scratch Golfer.
Route B: Handicap Golfer.

The bunkers in the middle of the fairway today were added during the Second World War to prevent enemy aircraft landing

The sixteenth on the East course. Not exactly as architect Harry Colt planned it but still a great hole

Nor was his work limited to Britain. On the Continent, he designed a number of famous courses including Eindhoven and Kennemer in The Netherlands and St Cloud and St Germain on the outskirts of Paris. In 1913, he travelled to the United States where he acted as a consultant for George Crump during the building of the renowned Pine Valley course in New Jersey.

A glance at the above list of his courses reveals that Colt had been involved in a number of projects on the heathlands of Surrey long before Tarrant brought him to Wentworth. In Wentworth's case, the land was ideal on which to build a golf course and, to his eternal credit, Colt took full advantage of that.

It is a tribute to the durability of his handiwork that 70 years after the job was finished much of his original course at Wentworth is still in play. What changes have been made, have been mostly superficial.

Altogether sixteen of the original holes remain much the same as they were in 1924, fifteen of them can be found on what has become the East course and the sixteenth is the first on the West which was started in 1925 and completed little more than twelve months later. It is not clear how much was spent on the original eighteen holes but the minutes of Club meetings at the time do reveal that a budget of £5,000 was laid aside for the West course. In an age when some top courses can cost as much as £40 million to build, a sum of £5,000 might not sound much but at the time it was sufficient to cause considerable disquiet among a group of senior members. Much to his chagrin, Colt was called on to itemize the costs involved and in the end it was only with Tarrant's support that he forced the budget through.

A map which was produced at the time, and which still hangs in the clubhouse, reveals that Colt's original eighteen holes measured 6,377 yards from the championship tees and a rather less demanding 5,470 yards from the forward tees. If the current set of measurement standards had applied at the time, the course would have had a par of 70 and would have featured twelve par 4s, four par 3s and two par 5s. The longest hole measured a formidable 610 yards from the 'tiger' tees and the shortest was a mere 119 yards from the forward tees.

Wentworth aficionados will be interested to learn that Colt's original course at Wentworth started with what is now the first hole on the West course. The second was another par 4 which started from a tee near to the first green and ended on the current first green on the East course. Thereafter, it followed much the same route as the existing East course although when the second eighteen holes were opened in 1926 the long 610 yards seventh hole was divided into two to enable the original first hole to be incorporated into the new eighteen.

Unfortunately, much less precise information survives about the

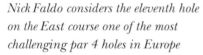

Nick Faldo considers the eleventh hole on the East course one of the most challenging par 4 holes in Europe

The eleventh hole on the West course played across a valley

VOLVO P.G.A. CHAMPIONSHIP 1991

DATE 24.5.91 TIME 11.10 ENTRY NO. Handicaps Strokes Rec'd PAR 73 SSS 73 / PAR 73 SSS 73

Player A WAYNE RILEY.

Marker's Score	Hole	White Yards	Par	Yellow Yards	Stroke Index	Score A	Score B	Nett Score	W=+ L=- H=0	Red Yards	Par	Stroke Index
	1	471	5	462	9	4				425	5	9
	2	155	3	137	17	3				121	3	17
	3	452	4	447	3	4				376	4	3
	4	501	5	479	11	3				421	5	11
	5	191	3	167	15	3				143	3	15
	6	344	4	328	13	4				310	4	13
	7	399	4	362	5	3				333	4	5
	8	398	4	389	7	4				346	4	7
	9	450	4	435	1	3				423	5	1
	OUT	3361	36	3206		31				2898	37	

PLEASE AVOID SLOW PLAY AT ALL TIMES

	10	186	3	177	10	3				174	3	10
	11	376	4	371	6	4				318	4	6
	12	483	5	468	14	3				418	5	14
	13	441	4	423	2	3				409	5	2
	14	179	3	179	18	3				117	3	18
	15	466	4	458	4	4				405	4	4
	16	380	4	369	16	3				352	4	16
	17	571	5	538	8	5				174	5	8
	18	502	5	486	12	4				458	5	12
	IN	3584	37	3469		32				3114	38	
	OUT	3361	36	3206		31				2898	37	
	TOTAL	6945	73	6675		63				6044	75	

STABLEFORD POINTS OR NETT RESULT HANDICAP NETT

Copyright Eagle Promotions 081-771 7321

Markers Signature ...RONALD J. STELTON... Players Signature ...Wayne Riley...

Wayne Riley's record 63 on the West

PICCADILLY TOURNAMENT

DATE 1964 TIME ENTRY NO. Handicaps Strokes Rec'd PAR 68 SSS 70 ✓ / PAR 68 SSS 69

Player A DOUG N SEWELL

Marker's Score	Hole	White Yards	Par	Yellow Yards	Stroke Index	Score A	Score B	Nett Score	W=+ L=- H=0	Red Yards	Par	Stroke Index
	1	391	4	379	11	3				351	4	5
	2	421	4	418	4	3				399	5	13
	3	337	4	325	13	3				292	4	8
	4	192	3	157	8	3				149	3	15
	5	327	4	295	17	3				283	4	10
	6	353	4	342	5	3				302	4	2
	7	229	3	217	15	3				178	3	12
	8	458	4	439	1	6				401	5	17
	9	531	5	499	9	4				469	5	4
	OUT	3239	35	3071		30				2824	37	

PLEASE AVOID SLOW PLAY AT ALL TIMES

	10	187	3	173	14	3				143	3	16
	11	462	4	460	3	4				404	4	1
	12	157	3	153	18	3				132	3	18
	13	402	4	389	6	3				327	4	3
	14	303	4	299	16	4				281	4	14
	15	332	4	327	10	4				294	4	6
	16	458	4	458	2	4				408	5	11
	17	213	3	213	12	3				195	3	9
	18	423	4	406	7	4				387	5	7
	IN	2937	33	2878		32				2571	35	
	OUT	3239	35	3071		30				2824	37	
	TOTAL	6176	68	5949		62				5349	72	

STABLEFORD POINTS OR NETT RESULT HANDICAP NETT

Copyright Eagle Promotions 081-771 7321

Markers Signature ...M Henry... Players Signature ...D. Sewell...

Doug Sewell's record 62 on the East

The eighth hole on the West is one of the most picturesque and the only one with water guarding the green

course which has come to be called the West and which is the regular venue for both the Volvo PGA Championship and the World Match-play Championship. We do know that its route has not been altered much since Colt pegged it out and that at one time it had no less than seven holes which under current measurement guidelines would be classified as par 5s, but that is about all. No such thing as a map of the course exists. All cards have disappeared. Indeed, much of the information that is left seems contradictory at first sight. A number of

references do survive from the 1920s which suggest that the course was considered difficult but it has also been documented that in 1938 former Open champion Alf Perry won the Dunlop Metropolitan tournament round the West course with four rounds under 70.

It is a tribute to the immense talent of the architect that both his creations have stood the test of time since the first seeds were sown. Technology might have advanced a great deal since Colt was in his prime, but it has not swamped two of his most enduring designs.

The Courses

Another Gem

JOHN WHITBREAD

How do you create a match for two masterpieces in your own back yard? That was the magnitude of the task that faced the Wentworth Club when they decided to build a third eighteen hole course to complement the already internationally famous West and East designed in the 1920s by Harry Colt.

The chance to build a third course arose because in 1978 Wentworth acquired around 150 acres of land between Wentworth and Sunningdale, an area known as The Great Wood. Before any decisions were taken on how to proceed with the South course, as it was originally known, Club officials made a series of fact-finding missions to courses in the United States including the Inverness and Muirfield Village Clubs in Ohio, Seminole and Sawgrass in Florida,

John Jacobs (centre) with his two design consultants, Gary Player (right) and Bernard Gallacher

and Augusta National in Georgia. The quality of the layouts and the facilities were carefully studied.

Previous applications to develop land on the estate had run into ecological and planning problems. The first concept for a totally separate £2 million public golf centre had met with strong opposition from neighbouring residents and the local Runnymede Borough Council. That plan had envisaged an eighteen hole layout plus a par 3 course with its own driving range, clubhouse and a separate entrance from Chobham Common. That having failed, the new Wentworth plan was simply to build an eighteen hole Club Members' course and integrate it with existing facilities. There would be no separate clubhouse or entrance.

In order to give the new planning application every chance of being passed by the local authority, Wentworth brought together a team of professional advisors to assist throughout the planning, design and construction stages. In addition to a planning consultant for the whole project, there was an environmental consultant to help the golf course architect.

John Jacobs Associates won the competition to build the course with a design that preserved as many specimen trees and retained as many natural features as possible. Gary Player, who had played in 20

John Jacobs Golf Associates'
pictorial plan of the new course

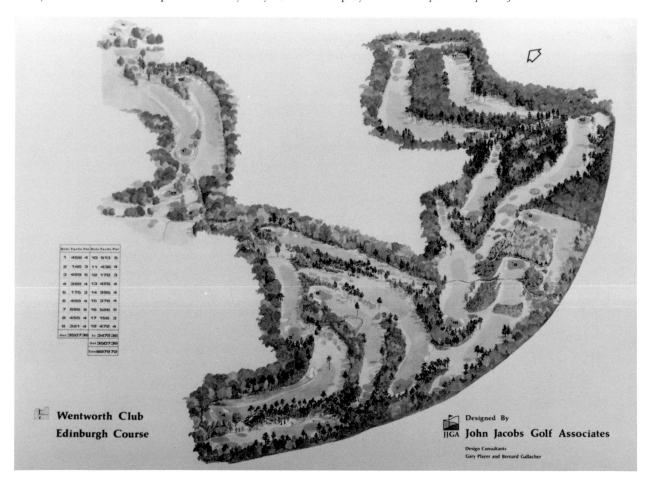

(Right) Richard Doyle-Davidson, Wentworth Club Secretary 1977-91, whose determination and drive brought the concept of the third course to completion, watches the work progressing

consecutive World Match-play Championships, and Club Professional Bernard Gallacher were added to the design team as consultants.

Experts from the Sports Turf Research Institute were brought in to advise the team on the specifications that should be sought for the new course. Representatives of the Surrey Wildlife Trust indicated three main areas of ecological importance that should be left untouched in the development of the new course. A video was made to stress the value of building a third course and to allay public fears

How the courses protect nature

Far from destroying animal, plant and bird life, it is now accepted that a golf course can protect them. In some cases, golf courses can even prove beneficial to nature's creatures. Playing round and worrying about your swing, your lost putting stroke or your score, you may not have time nor the inclination to notice the wild life around

Hobbies were found nesting in pine trees at the third hole of the Edinburgh course after tree clearing operations

you. But it is there – in the air, in the trees and bushes, on the grass and under the ground, in the ponds, everywhere. These days, with proper planning, golf courses – and there are nearly five hundred square miles of them in Britain – are natural sanctuaries for Britain's flora and fauna.

When the Environmental Advisory Unit of the Department of Botany at the University of Liverpool did an exhaustive ecological survey and assessment of the land over which the new Edinburgh course was being built a few years ago, the researchers identified as residents of the Wentworth Estate almost 60 different types of bird. These included nuthatch, great spotted woodpecker and treecreeper in the woodlands along with blackcap and goldcrest, dunnock and robin whose territories can be more extensive. Tree and meadow tits, pied wagtails, bullfinch and chaffinch, the song thrush and blackbird were all among those carefully noted along with heron from the heronry at nearby Fort Belvedere, nightingale, willow warbler, moorhen, pheasant, mandarin duck and pigeon. In short, a veritable kaleidoscope of birds of all sizes and colours

about how the environment and the wild life on the site might be affected.

All the preparations to ensure the application to build would be passed had been extensive and were ultimately successful. The Club's application had also been strengthened by the fact that one of the most sensitive areas, which had been highlighted by the ecologists as worth preserving but which also happened to be ideal for golf course development, was not included in the final plan.

So aware were the Club officials about maintaining, indeed

(Above left)
The fourth hole takes shape

(Above) Bulldozers moving earth at the eighteenth. Such work for Colt's designs for the East and West would have all been carried out by manual labour

and with very distinctive habits make their homes happily on the Wentworth estate.

The research showed that no truly rare species were inhabitants but wood warblers, local to Surrey, breed in the area as do sparrowhawks which hunt along the woodland edges and find Wentworth an ideal hunting ground. The vegetation of the estate – a mixture of woodlands, wooded gardens, managed seminatural grasslands and heaths – means the estate is good for all wild life but especially for birds.

Centuries ago, the whole area was probably covered by woodland so it is no surprise that there are many different species of tree in the Club's large blocks of woodlands and woodland strips. In particular, there are birch, alder, Scots pine and beech which provide the main canopy, with holly and sweet chestnut providing an occasional second layer. In some areas the vegetation includes well developed rowan, sycamore, various types of oak, grey willow and alder.

Ancient woodland has a much richer and more diverse ground flora than younger woodlands and Wentworth is dominated to a large extent by bracken,

honeysuckle and bramble, redcurrant, wood sage, cleavers and fern. There is plenty of heather and bell heather, most of it on heathland such as the Broomhall Common, the most important seminatural habitat on the Wentworth estate. It has been designated as a Site of Special Scientific Interest.

By retaining most of the valuable woodland and ensuring the preservation of certain specimen trees, Wentworth's specially commissioned study ensured that the ecology of the area was not damaged when the Edinburgh course was built.

At the eleventh hole on the new course there are over 20 tall herb grasses and a further ten varieties of the plant are to be found around the fourteenth and fifteenth. All the natural growth on the golf courses is backed up by the more sophisticated cultivation of private house gardens.

The Club's provision of a dedicated nature reserve managed by the Surrey Wildlife Trust is further proof of Wentworth's determination to ensure that what has been an idyllic home for so many animals will continue to be so.

A stream runs in front of the green at the short second hole

improving, the balance of nature in the area that 60 acres were designated at that time as the Wentworth Nature Reserve. The layout for the new 7,000 yard par 72 course, designed by former Ryder Cup Captain John Jacobs, was also influenced by a twelve month study of the site between Knowle Green and Longcross Station conducted by the Department of Botany at Liverpool University.

Planning permission was granted in August 1986 and just a month later John Jacobs held his first site meeting with his design consultants. Even at that first meeting, with The Great Wood still virgin territory, their enthusiasm for the project was unmistakeable.

The autumn storm of 1987, the worst for over two hundred years, brought down trees that Jacobs had singled out for preservation as vital to the layout. Disappointing though that was, work began enthusiastically in March 1988 on the course which would match, in every respect, Colt's two designs.

'Wentworth has to be one of the best golfing sites in the world,' enthused Player. 'I have said before that I would be happy in my retirement to come back and just walk the West course; it is so beautiful. To be given the chance to match it is really thrilling. The land here is so right that if we cannot create something truly memorable we should never be given another golf course to work on again.'

Those sentiments were echoed by John Jacobs who declared: 'We have a wonderful setting in Great Wood but our big test will be to design the best possible opening and finishing holes which need to be built away from the main area of development.' Added Gallacher: 'I am not an experienced architect like the other two but I am on the spot and I do know the feel and history of the place. I hope I can help build a course of which Wentworth can be proud.'

The problem, highlighted by Jacobs, of linking the clubhouse with the main body of the course in Great Wood was solved by taking over four holes of Wentworth's highly popular short course.

Following the initial site meeting, a full topographical survey was

From behind the green at the testing par 3 fifth hole

made and superimposed on the original plan, showing important physical features and specimen trees which the Club were keen to maintain.

In September 1987 the design team met again to plot the final route of the eighteen holes and by early 1988 they were able to walk the proposed fairways on land from which 1,500 tons of wood had been removed in a remarkable clearance operation achieved in record time by a team of New Zealand lumberjacks assigned to the job. All the work was done in detailed consultation with the project's Environmental Advisory Unit from Liverpool University, the Wentworth Estate's Road Committee, the Runnymede Borough Council and the Surrey Wildlife Trust.

That muddy march through Great Wood on a bitterly cold winter's morning did nothing to dim the team's expectations! Player, eyes sparkling with delight, strode out ahead of the official party exclaiming: 'The 500 yards third hole with its superb trees and natural bankings and the short fifth with its great contours are particularly exciting.'

Jacobs agreed, pointing out that a large part of the architects' work had been made much easier by virtue of the superb piece of ground they had been blessed to work with.

Back in the clubhouse Jacobs summed up the architects' thoughts: 'We believe we have now found the right balance that will suit golfers of all capabilities and that, if all goes to plan, the eighteenth, in particular, will be a memorable closing hole with a huge banked amphitheatre surrounding the green.'

While the design demanded extensive tree clearance, very little earth movement was required. The exceptions were at the first where the raised green of the old short course first hole was levelled, and at the stunning 420 yards par 4 fourth hole where a huge cutting was made through an earth bank where the hole doglegs right to drop dramatically to a tree-lined green.

By March 1988, the main contractors had moved in and within six months fourteen fairways had been completed and seeded. In September of that year, 33,000 square yards of turf (enough to cover four football pitches) were laid on the tees and greens, turf which had been grown on a special sand base near to the Turf Institute headquarters at Bingley. This turf was laid on painstakingly prepared sand surfaces.

By April 1989, John Jacobs was like a painter constantly seeking to find perfection on his latest canvas, seeing something to improve upon every time he set foot on the new creation.

The second hole, as Jacobs readily admits, owes much to the famous twelfth at Augusta. A stream that was an unused feature on the short course was diverted to weave in front of the new wide but shallow green. A deep bunker in the face and at the rear of the raised right half of the green makes pin placement all important.

'It spells out the ethos of our whole design in that it can be relatively easy playing from the front tees to a generous pin placement or it can be made progressively harder to suit all occasions,' explained Jacobs.

Apart from the second and the seventeenth, where you have to play over a beautiful lake to a kidney shaped green, water has been used sparingly but very cleverly, on the eighth and fifteenth. At the eighth, the stream which ran in front of the green has been diverted to flow 50 yards short of the putting surface giving the player a choice; whether to lay up with the second shot or go for the green. On the fifteenth, the creek has again been diverted to run across the fairway, some 240 yards from the back tee.

'This hole is played into the prevailing wind so it means that whatever standard of player you are, playing off whatever tee, the challenge of whether or not to try and drive the creek will be there,' explained Jacobs.

Building the new South course was a feat of engineering, logistics, finance and creativity but all man's ingenuity has to be tempered by the laws of nature.

The great gales of October 1987 – the worst in over one hundred years – destroyed several prime specimen trees and two very dry summers in succession delayed the original opening to July 1990 – eighteen months later than planned.

(Below left) Diagram showing the diversion of the stream (A) to (B) in the design of the Edinburgh eighth and fifteenth holes

(Below) The Edinburgh course card. All the par 3s were iron shots by design following up on Harry Colt's strategy for the East and West courses. Gary Orr's record 67 was achieved in the Peugeot Cup of 1991

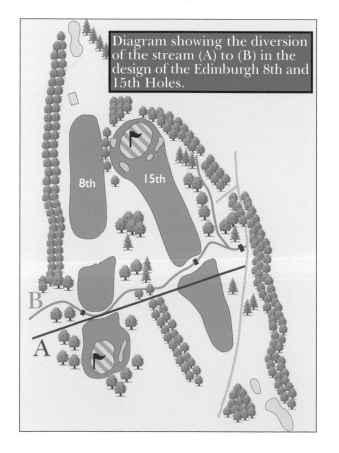

Diagram showing the diversion of the stream (A) to (B) in the design of the Edinburgh 8th and 15th Holes.

COMPETITION	PEUGEOT CUP

DATE 20 AUGUST 1991 TIME 11.45 ENTRY NO.

PlayerA GARY ORR

PlayerB

Marker's Score	Hole	White Yards	Par	Yellow Yards	Stroke Index	Score A	Score B	Nett Score	W = + L = - H = 0	Red Yards	Par	Stroke Index
	1	458	4	434	7	5				404	5	11
	2	146	3	127	17	3				106	3	15
	3	499	5	476	3	4				417	5	9
	4	399	4	365	11	4				332	4	3
	5	175	3	157	13	3				129	3	17
	6	459	4	421	1	4				370	4	5
	7	595	5	551	9	5				449	5	7
	8	455	4	425	5	3				366	4	1
	9	321	4	289	15	4				261	4	13
OUT		3507	36	3245		35				2834	37	

PLEASE AVOID SLOW PLAY AT ALL TIMES

	10	513	5	476	12	3				399	5	12
	11	436	4	417	2	4				370	4	2
	12	170	3	152	16	3				125	3	18
	13	426	4	407	6	4				359	4	4
	14	395	4	376	10	4				359	4	10
	15	378	4	356	14	4				304	4	6
	16	526	5	503	4	4				422	5	14
	17	156	3	140	18	2				95	3	16
	18	472	4	445	8	4				418	5	8
IN		3472	36	3272		32				2857	37	
OUT		3507	36	3245		35				2834	37	
TOTAL		6979	72	6517		67				5691	74	

67

STABLEFORD POINTS OR NETT RESULT	HANDICAP
	NETT

Copyright Eagle Promotions 081-771 7321

Holes won ....
Holes lost ....
Result ....

Markers Signature C anakens

Players Signature Gy ORR

Please indicate which tee used.

PAR 72 SSS 73
PAR 72 SSS 71

The tee shot at the attractive short seventeenth hole is played over water

The stylish tee-marker at the Edinburgh course's first hole

By the time the Duke of Edinburgh conducted the opening ceremony for a South course now renamed the Edinburgh course in his honour, it was already winning generous accolades from members and visitors alike.

One man who was particularly proud to see the South course dream become reality was Richard Doyle-Davidson who, at various times in his roles as Club Secretary, Managing Director and Special Projects Director, had witnessed every stage of its development.

'We had a tremendously hard act to follow but I believe our architects read the piece of land on which the course is built beautifully. The new course fits in so well with the West and East, yet without being a copy of either of them. Each hole is self contained and has its own individuality. It may only be a couple of years old but already there is a great feeling of history and space. They have taken the superb traditional concepts used to make the West and East and by incorporating modern ideas and using the most up to date construction methods have given us a gem. Now the club has three great courses to meet the modern golfing boom.'

*HRH the Duke of Edinburgh after
unveiling the memorial stone, accompanied
by Elliott Bernerd, Chairman of the
Wentworth Club*

*(Below) The view from behind the green of
the dogleg thirteenth*

The Ryder Cup

MICHAEL WILLIAMS

The solid gold cup donated by Samuel Ryder

Had it not been for the Royal & Ancient Golf Club's decision to stage a regional qualifying round for the 1926 Open Championship there might never have been a Ryder Cup. By such matters of chance, which earlier had involved a stubborn father, an ambitious son and lastly a chance remark in the bar of the Wentworth Golf Club, did destiny take hold.

One of those regional qualifying rounds was held at Sunningdale and was dominated by Bobby Jones. His 66, which contained 33 shots, 33 putts, 33 out and 33 back, is still held as one of the most impressive model rounds ever played. A week later, he travelled to Royal Lytham, won the Open and in the Club's homage had a plaque set at the back of a fairway bunker on the seventeenth hole to mark the spot from where he played the shot that decided the Championship.

There had, nevertheless, been an interval between the regional qualifying round and the Championship itself and, for want of something to do, the professionals trooped down the A30 to Wentworth for an informal match between the British and the visiting Americans.

They played it on what is now the East course and the British repeated a victory they had at Gleneagles Hotel in Scotland in 1921, winning by a thumping margin of 13½ – 1½. Two of those points came from Abe Mitchell. He beat Jim Barnes, who a year earlier had won the Open at Prestwick, by 8 and 7 which was only marginally less severe than the 9 and 8 drubbing he and George Duncan had inflicted on Barnes and the great Walter Hagen in the foursomes.

It also happened that Mitchell, said to be the best British golfer never to win the Open, was personal tutor to one of the most enthusiastic spectators, a small, elderly man who had made a fortune selling penny packets of seeds to the garden–lovers of England. His name was Samuel Ryder. He was first into the bar afterwards to buy drinks all round!

Amid the banter, Ryder happened to remark: 'We should do this again.' It did not fall on deaf ears. He was at once prevailed upon to donate a cup. It was small, elegant and made of gold. It cost £250 and the figure on the lid was modelled on Mitchell. Thus, the Ryder Cup match was born. A year later the cup was in the hands of the Americans who swamped the British 9½ – 2½ at Worcester, Massachusetts, a pattern that until recent years was not unusual

Samuel Ryder did not take up golf until he was past his 50th birthday. He was the son of a Manchester corn merchant but his father was suspicious of his son trying to sell seeds. Consequently, the young man moved south at the end of the 1800s to set up his own business, the Heath and Heather Company in St Albans. Success was instant and with wealth came more leisure time. He joined the Verulam Club in 1910, became Captain in little more than a year and in 1923 sponsored a Heath and Heather professional tournament, one of the first of its kind. He was a genuine golfing enthusiast.

Ryder's affinity with Mitchell probably had something to do with the fact that the professional had once been a gardener. Ryder appointed him his private professional at £1,000 a year, a considerable sum in those days, and it was only natural that he wanted Mitchell to be the first British Ryder Cup Captain. Unfortunately, however, Mitchell fell ill before the team sailed for the States although he did play in the next three matches.

By the time the Ryder Cup came to Wentworth in 1953 for the first and only occasion, both Ryder and Mitchell had died, Ryder in 1936 at the age of 78 and Mitchell in 1947. The match itself was not

Samuel Ryder, the St Albans seed merchant and mad-keen golf enthusiast, who employed Abe Mitchell as his private professional, donated the Ryder Cup for a biennial match between the professionals of Great Britain & Ireland and the USA

Some members of the 1927 British Ryder Cup team at Waterloo en route to America. Most of them had played in the unofficial match at Wentworth in 1926. Samuel Ryder – donor of the Cup – was there to see them off. No one can remember the name of the dog!

Ben Hogan, now 80, won the
US Masters, the US Open and The
Open in 1953 but missed the Ryder Cup

exactly healthy either! The then combined British and Irish team had won the first two home matches at Moortown in 1929 and at Southport and Ainsdale in 1933. In those days, the home side always had an advantage over an away team desperately trying to find land legs after the week-long sea crossing. By 1953, the overall match score was, however, 7-2 to the United States.

Nonetheless, this was a year of optimism and celebration. The memory of the war and rationing was fading. Elizabeth was crowned Queen and there was a new bounce in the national step. John Hunt (now Lord Hunt of Llanfair) led the successful ascent of Everest. England's cricketers beat the Australians to take the Ashes. Gordon Richards, later knighted for his contribution to horse racing, won his first Derby. Stanley Matthews, later Sir Stanley, won his first FA Cup-winners medal and tennis star Jaraslov Drobny, the popular Czech, won Wimbledon.

That summer, Ben Hogan also won the Open at Carnoustie but he was not in the Ryder Cup team. After his car accident he was no longer keen to play 36 holes a day for two days. That was still the traditional format, four foursomes on the first day and eight singles the following day. Hogan's absence was seen as a decided advantage to the British cause. The 1953 US line-up was not regarded as a vintage American team even if it did include Sam Snead.

There were those who felt that Henry Cotton, the home Captain, although now 46, should have been in the Great Britain & Ireland team. Bernard Hunt, who was in the side, recalls him in a practice round 'cutting up a little wood' from a downhill lie to the green at the seventh that was beyond the scope of any of the team he led. However, doctors had ruled that Cotton, whose health was seldom robust,

Young Bernard Hunt desperately
disappointed because of missing the
final putt which would have won him
his game and given Britain & Ireland
a drawn match

should stick to his nonplaying role, and he took their advice.

If the stars of the zodiac, which shone so brightly on sporting achievement in this year of the Coronation, were seen by some as an indication that the Ryder Cup was about to come home again, the prognostication proved to be so nearly, so tantalisingly correct. The match will be remembered for ever as the one that was there for the taking but which, because of two slips by the two youngest members of the Great Britain & Ireland team, ended in the narrowest of defeats, 6½ – 5½.

The two unfortunates were Hunt, then 23, and Peter Alliss, 22. The one over par 6s both took at the final hole when 5s would have done were something with which they have had to live ever since, just as those who were there to witness the drama at Wentworth that afternoon still shudder at the memory.

For all that, it was a stirring recovery for Great Britain & Ireland, so used to defeat, to come so near to winning. Nevertheless, the foursomes were an immense disappointment to the daily ten thousand strong crowds who came to watch and to the first ever television audience, two million strong. No golf event had ever received such extensive exposure on the screen before. It was all too much for one man. Raymond Oppenheimer was to be a part of the broadcasting

Sam Snead playing from a bunker apparently unconcerned by the close proximity of cameramen and spectators

The First Tented Village

One reporter began his 1953 Ryder Cup story: 'I am phoning this from a new town which has sprung up almost overnight amid the trees and shrubs at Wentworth. It has a bank, a post office, radio and newspaper offices, restaurants, cloakrooms, bars and even a row of shops. It is a town of great marquees set on the emerald green of the majestic course on which the Ryder Cup match begins tomorrow.'

He had every right to be suitably impressed. The arrangements made by the Club and the Professional Golfers' Association were quite simply brilliant. In particular, Wentworth excelled itself by setting new spectator viewing standards which others would later try to emulate.

In his story, the suitably impressed reporter pointed out that there were half-a-dozen car parks capable of accommodating 12,000 cars and an army of 1,100 volunteer stewards from eighteen different clubs in the area, all of whom had been training for three months, who were ready to handle the expected 20,000 spectators with maximum efficiency.

In charge of the grand strategy on the West course was Major Peter Roscow, the Wentworth Club Secretary. He had set himself the task of doing even better than the officials at Ganton had done in 1949. He controlled the operation with military efficiency. In case of trouble, he had four emergency squads patrolling the four zones into which he had divided the course. They were controlled by 'watchers' who could signal instantly for assistance if it was required by hoisting telescopic poles on top of which were what Roscow called SOS boards which were white.

Scouts, coordinated by Chief Steward, Douglas Caird, who could only do his job properly by using a motor cycle, went ahead of each match giving stewarding crews a 20-minute warning of the arrival of the players.

Professional golfers were drafted in by Major Roscow not only to advise the signallers sending scores back to base by walkie-talkie but also to act as bodyguards for the contestants. They fended off autograph hunters! As further player protection, the tees were fenced off with chestnut paling to give them room to drive. Twelve miles of red twine was used to prevent the crowds from encroaching on the fairways.

Major Roscow also imposed what he described as a 'silence zone' at the busy junction where the seventh and tenth greens are in close proximity to the eighth and eleventh tees. Spectators in this area were expressly forbidden to cheer for fear of distracting another game! Those were the days!

Douglas Caird, the Chief Steward, moved round the course at speed controlling the galleries

Mel the cartoonist at his best. All the 1953 Ryder Cup players appear in happy mood, including Bernard Hunt and Peter Alliss but Henry Cotton, the nonplaying Captain, appears to be expecting to lose the match

team but found he could not climb the steep ladder to the commentary box and withdrew his services!

The foursomes were lost 3 – 1, the point coming from the two Irishmen, Fred Daly and Harry Bradshaw. According to Desmond Hackett in the *Daily Express*, the six-foot putt Daly holed on the last green to beat Walter Burkemo and Cary Middlecoff resulted in 'the sweetest sound all day'. Daly had a routine of passing the putter head backwards and forwards over the ball before actually striking it. Hunt recalls standing by the green and counting twelve passes.

Nevertheless, Cotton was angered by his team's performance and gave them quite a dressing down. This should have been a private affair but clearly there was a 'leak'! The Press got hold of the story and printed it the following morning. 'Cotton kicks Ryder Cup members' blazed the placards of the more restrained tabloids of those days.

The 'don't mince words' pep talk Cotton gave the team had the necessary galvanizing effect even though Dai Rees, who had been left out of the foursomes, lost the top single to Jack Burke. Daly held his form of the previous day and ran away from Ted Kroll by 9 and 7. Then came another point from the determinedly patriotic Eric Brown who began his 100 per cent singles record in four Cup matches by beating Lloyd Mangrum two up.

However, it was Harry Weetman playing in a necktie who suddenly gave the Great Britain & Ireland fans genuine hope that overall victory was possible when, from four down and six to play, he came through to a remarkable victory against Snead. Though 1951 Open

PICTURES OF THE WEEK

Our roving cameras cover the current golfing scene

Top left: Distinguished visitors at Wentworth were Mr. Winthrop Aldridge, the American Ambassador, and his wife. With them are Harry Radix, of the American P.G.A. (*left*) and Henry Cotton.

Top right: Cary Middlecoff and Walter Burkemo find trouble at the third hole in their foursomes match. They eventually lost on the last green to Daly and Bradshaw.

Left: Ryder Cup team manager, Fred Corcoran (*right*), with chairman of the U.S.P.G.A., Joe Novak.

Right: Bob Hope rooting for his country at Wentworth has a chat with Jim Turnesa after the first round of his singles match with Peter Alliss.

Bottom left: Fred Daly, hero of the Ryder Cup matches, has a police escort as he walks off the last green.

Below: Harry Weetman and his wife leave the last green hand in hand after Harry's one hole victory over Sam Snead.

Bottom right: Eric Brown plays to the ninth green overlooked by the television tower.

For Golf Illustrated *the Ryder Cup was big news*

champion, Max Faulkner was about to go down to Middlecoff. Alliss, one up with three to play against Jim Turnesa, and Hunt, ultimately one up with one to play against Dave Douglas, could still do it. The task lay heavy on their young shoulders.

But Alliss lost both the sixteenth and seventeenth where he drove out of bounds and then missed a golden opportunity of taking the eighteenth for what would have been a halved game. Turnesa was in trouble off the tee and was always taking 6. Alliss, who was just wide of the green in 2, fluffed a little pitch, chipped again, missed the putt and lost.

Right behind him came Hunt, and there was more anguish for the home galleries. A half in five would have meant a tied match. Instead, the young Briton, like Alliss making his Ryder Cup debut, three-putted for a 6, lost the hole to a 5 by Douglas and only halved his game. The Ryder Cup remained in American custody.

It had all been so agonizingly near but so far! Four years on, however, the match would go to Lindrick near Sheffield and that would be a much happier story.

Wentworth, where the match had been given its official stamp with the presentation of the Cup, had proved itself as a championship course of quality that provided a stern test for the best players in the world.

Placards angered Captain's wife

Mrs Henry Cotton created quite a stir at the 1953 Ryder Cup when her husband was Captain. While the crowds waited in the mist at Wentworth for play to start, she caused a diversion when she walked up to a newspaper stand in front of the clubhouse, ripped down a newspaper placard and tore it to pieces.

She explained the reason for her anger to the astonished crowd: 'I tore it down because it tells lies. All the newspapers except one have told lies about Henry today and should be ashamed of themselves.' She was referring to a news agency report which had quoted Cotton as saying, after the first day when his Great Britain & Ireland side lost three of the four foursomes: 'I am ashamed of the way our fellows played.'

Later, Cotton told reporters: 'I feel that I have been misquoted, I did not intend to suggest that I was ashamed of any member of the British team but I was disappointed with some of the golf in general.'

Mrs 'Toots' Cotton

The Curtis Cup

ROBERT GREEN

Unlike many longer established clubs, Wentworth has never been a bastion of male chauvinism. It will come as no surprise, therefore, to learn that the first official Curtis Cup match between the lady amateurs of America and a team of ladies representing the four Home Countries was played over the Club's delightful East course in 1932.

These days, the Curtis Cup is a fixture which, like the men's professional match between Europe and America for the Ryder Cup, is always a closely contested affair. In 1964, Henry Longhurst, the famous writer and commentator, had these erudite words to say after watching the Curtis Cup match at Royal Porthcawl:

'To the true lover of golf I found myself recapturing all the old excitement when watching the match at Royal Porthcawl. The fact is that given a reasonable course, the best of the women play just as well

as the men and are a good deal more decorative. The girls play at a lively speed and in the best possible spirit and if you want to watch golf at its best then go and watch a Curtis Cup match.'

Praise, indeed, for a match which after a series of 'friendlies' became official at Wentworth 61 years ago. At the time, the Club regularly hosted golfing 'occasions' as part of the publicity campaign to increase public awareness of the new, impressive golfing complex with its substantial, well-built homes and plots on which to build others.

The chance to return to Wentworth for the 60th anniversary match was missed by the Ladies' Golf Union, but there is still a modern day link between the match and the Club. Bernard Gallacher, the Club Professional, is – and has been for several years – the Great Britain & Ireland Curtis Cup team's official coach.

Just like the Ryder Cup, it took a series of unofficial matches to get the real thing off the ground. Even then, it was the presentation of a handsome trophy for biennial transatlantic competition by two American golfing sisters, Harriot and Margaret Curtis, after one of those unofficial matches that helped give the fixture the permanence it now enjoys. But, initially, it seemed doomed never to get going.

The late Douglas Caird, a specialist on women's golf in Britain, has charted the events that led eventually to the development of the match. It makes fascinating reading.

Initial interest had been shown in 1905 with a fixture at Royal Cromer between the home players and those American golfers who had made what was then a long and tiring sea crossing to compete for the women's amateur title that year. This fixture was billed as the United States versus England although the home side did include

The sisters Margaret and Harriot Curtis who conceived the match in 1905 when they played in the first unofficial USA versus Great Britain match, following the Ladies' Championship at Cromer. Through no fault of the sisters, but rather due to official dilatoriness, it took 37 years before the match was established properly

Wanda Morgan

ON DOUBLE DUTY

If golf has changed over the years, and it has, then so has golf writing. The following are extracts from the Golf Illustrated *report of the first Curtis Cup match, held on Wentworth's East course in May 1932.*

'Before the largest crowd that has yet attended a London course – it must have numbered fully 10,000...' (Pre-World Match-play days, remember) ... 'America beat Britain...' (Nothing revolutionary there) ... 'In the morning she won all three of the foursomes...' (Sorry, she?) ... 'gave her a total of five matches against Britain's three...' (Her?) These days, golf teams from the United States are either 'it' or 'them' but then Wanda Morgan was not writing about golf today. And the above was only part of her first paragraph. She went on: 'The American team played jolly good golf, and that is all there is to it.' Even The Daily Telegraph *would* consider altering that offering from one of its correspondents. The next sentence continued: 'We should have had to have been on our very best behaviour to have saved the day (All of us?), and some of us were not.' In case you're wondering, that meant that some of the players were not on top form, rather than that they broke a few clubs, ignored a team curfew or got the worse for wear on kummel.

But Wanda Morgan was not only writing about the Curtis Cup. She had been playing in it. The previous year, she had been beaten in the final of the Ladies' British Amateur (which she was to win in 1935) and that same summer she had won the first of the three English Ladies' titles she was to collect. Wanda Morgan was a fine golfer.

And in this first Curtis Cup, her foursomes partner was the British Captain, Joyce Wethered, four times British and five times English champion. Already, she was recognized as perhaps the greatest woman golfer of all time. Certainly, she terrified her partner and scribe. Wrote Wanda: 'I was just terribly nervous. I know I should not have been. But the fact remains that I was, and I might just as well admit it. Why I was seized with this nervousness Heaven only knows. I had a genius for a partner. And yet that may have been the cause. I was so anxious not to let her down. And in my anxiety I did.'

(So that's clear, then. It was all Wanda's fault.)

'I see some of the critics have been inclined to blame Miss Wethered for our defeat in this first foursome,' added Miss Morgan. 'They are wrong...' (OK, so she's modest) ...

'Granted that Joyce never came within sight of the tremendously high standard she usually sets herself...' (OK, quite modest) ... 'these critics must remember she was carrying an awful weight in her partner!' (OK, insufferably modest.)

Despite further self-deprecation and fluffed shots from Miss Morgan ('We won the second, where both Mrs Hill and I had a top each...'), the match was all square playing the last, where 'we proceeded to lose this final hole to a 6!' Of course, that was mostly Wanda's fault, too. 'I started the rot with an appalling brassie shot...'

Mind you, Wanda had a disarmingly pleasant line in damning her team-mates. Commenting on the last hole defeat of Molly Gourlay and Doris Park, she noted: 'From the eighteenth tee Miss Park looked up long before her club reached the ball, and Miss Gourlay had to play the next from the semi-bog in front of the tee.'

Seldom can an outrageous top have been so genteelly chastised.

Scottish and Irish players as well. The well-known tennis player Lottie Dod captained England and was the only loser on the team! The Curtis sisters – Harriot who had won the US women's title in 1906 and Margaret, a three-times winner of the title between 1907 (when she met her sister in the final) and 1912 – were in the American line-up. They were so impressed by the spirit of the event that they offered to donate a cup 'to stimulate friendly relations between women golfers of many lands' – a somewhat grander ideal perhaps than Britain versus America but it was the latter interpretation that the British and American authorities finally adopted.

The original global idea was welcomed but there was one major stumbling block to such a fixture being established at that time. Money was the key, or rather, the lack of it was. Travel in those days was expensive and the idea of several nations competing prompted thoughts in the minds of officials not just of the cost but also of the months of painstaking preparation needed to make it work.

Britain versus America could be much more easily handled! Meeting after meeting was held to thrash out a formula for such a match but without a satisfactory result. The talks were continuing when, in 1911, another unofficial fixture was staged at Royal Portrush featuring America & the Colonies against Great Britain. As at Cromer, the home team won.

Still nothing had been decided about a more permanent fixture by the outbreak of the First World War and not much happened to sort things out in the years after the war. At Burnham and Berrow in 1923 the sides of yet another unofficial match were labelled, somewhat curiously. Overseas versus the Rest of England but it gave something of a boost to the smouldering idea of a regular match.

Then in 1930, 25 years after the Curtis sisters had offered their trophy, Glenna Collett Vare, one of America's greatest ever golfers, threw down a challenge to Joyce Wethered (now Lady Heathcot-Amory) to organize another 'friendly' between America and Great Britain & Ireland.

(Above left) The 1932 US team.
Front: Mrs Harley Higby,
Mrs L D Cheney.
Middle: Virginia Van Wie,
Helen Hicks, Glenna Collett Vare,
Marion Hollins (Captain)
Back: Maureen Orcutt, Opal Hill

(Above) The Great Britain & Ireland team.
Back: Enid Wilson, Wanda Morgan,
Diana Fishwick, Joyce Wethered
(Captain), Elsie Corlett
Front: Mrs J B Watson, Doris Park,
Molly Gourlay.

Cold and bedraggled ball markers make the best of the rainy weather. It appears that on this occasion Great Britain & Ireland outdrove the USA

Mrs Vare had been US champion six times, the Canadian title-holder twice and in successive years had lost in the final of the Women's Championship in Britain to Diana Fishwick (now Mrs A C Critchley) at Formby and then to Joyce Wethered at St Andrews.

Joyce Wethered, still regarded as one of the world's greatest women golfers, had won the British title four times, the English title five times and, with a string of partners, the famous Worplesdon Foursomes seven times. She decided that she did not want to organize the event and handed the job on to Molly Gourlay, twice English champion, three times the French and three times the Swedish title-holder and twice winner of the Belgian Women's Championship. Molly Gourlay, sadly now deceased, was still playing off 4 at the age of 73.

Without any help from the Ladies' Golf Union, Miss Gourlay set about the task of organizing the match with vim and gusto. She persuaded the Sunningdale Club to allow the match to be played over the famous Old course. Although the match was still 'unofficial,' the press and public interest in it was considerable. Uncharitably, the

Curtis Cup at Wentworth 1932

FOURSOMES

Joyce Wethered and Wanda Morgan	lost to	Glenna Collett Vare and Mrs Opal Hill by one hole
Enid Wilson and Mrs J B Watson	lost to	Virginia Van Wie and Helen Hicks 2 and 1
Molly Gourlay and Doris Park	lost to	Maureen Orcutt and Mrs L D Cheney by one hole
GREAT BRITAIN & IRELAND	0	USA 3

SINGLES

Joyce Wethered	beat	Glenna Collett Vare 6 and 4
Enid Wilson	beat	Helen Hicks 2 and 1
Wanda Morgan	lost to	Virginia Van Wie 2 and 1
Diana Fishwick	beat	Maureen Orcutt 4 and 3
Molly Gourlay	halved with	Mrs Opal Hill
Elsie Corlett	lost to	Mrs L D Cheney 4 and 3
GREAT BRITAIN & IRELAND	3½	USA 2½

Match Aggregate		
GREAT BRITAIN & IRELAND	3½	USA 5½

press considered that it would end in a huge defeat for the home ladies. Five thousand spectators came to watch. Reporters, photographers and even film cameramen were there to record the action and, in most cases, eat their words.

Miss Gourlay beat Glenna Collett Vare in the top match and inspired Great Britain & Ireland to a triumphant success. The result brought an official Curtis Cup match closer and in 1932, the seemingly reluctant LGU and the United States Golf Association, which organizes women's golf in America, agreed terms for a biennial meeting.

In May of that year, everyone gathered at Wentworth for the first official match and this time the Americans won all three foursomes and won, in the end, by two points. Joyce Wethered captained the Great Britain & Ireland team on this first official match and beat Glenna Collett Vare in the top singles. Former American champion Marion Hollins captained the American team in what was dubbed 'The Ladies' International Match'. Curiously, the trophy presented by the Curtis sisters to encourage the regular playing of the match was not on view but the fixture had been established, a fixture that is as popular today as ever. In fact, in 1958 the Curtis sisters offered to replace their original trophy with something altogether more grand but wisely, on sentimental grounds, this was turned down.

Today, despite the original concept of a World Cup, the match remains steadfastly Great Britain & Ireland versus America, the women amateurs refusing to go the way of their male professional colleagues whose Great Britain & Ireland Ryder Cup side has been transformed to one representing Europe.

Molly Gourlay (left) and Glenna Collett Vare meet during the Curtis Cup at Muirfield in 1984

Joyce Wethered driving, watched by Glenna Collett Vare (seated), Marion Hollins (US Captain) and Molly Gourlay (Great Britain & Ireland)

Lewine Mair, in her excellent book *One Hundred Years of Women's Golf* recalls that the American team for the first match at Wentworth stayed just a few miles from the course at the impressive Great Fosters Hotel with its tall Elizabethan-style chimneys. What surprised everyone was their dedicated pre-match practice. Since foursomes golf never has been played regularly in America, team Captain Hollins had the side playing every possible permutation of partnership in the days leading up to the fixture. With their extensive knowledge of the course, the Great Britain & Ireland girls not only did not practise, they only turned up for late afternoon tea the day before the match was due to start!

Enid Wilson, who played in the first Curtis Cup, remembers that both Captains were shocked at the pairings produced for the foursomes but that the American Captain had the last laugh when completing a first day foursomes whitewash of the home side.

Prior to the Second World War, the Americans won twice more but only drew at Gleneagles in 1936 when Jessie Anderson (later Mrs Jessie Valentine) on the first of her seven Cup appearances rammed in a monster putt on the last against Mrs L D Cheney to ensure the draw.

Post war, the Americans won in 1948 and 1950 but that year's heaviest defeat of the Great Britain & Ireland side at Buffalo when only 'Bunty' Stephens prevented a whitewash, was followed by a magnificent Great Britain & Ireland victory in 1952 at Muirfield. Great Britain & Ireland lost again at Merion in 1954 but won the trophy back in 1956 and kept a share of it in 1958 when the match was drawn for the second time.

There then followed thirteen straight American victories although they won only by a point in 1984 at Muirfield, and Molly Gourlay talked at the closing dinner for 30 minutes on the spirit shown by the players 50 years earlier to get the match established.

There was a new spirit around in the 1980s, too, and it fell to Mrs Diane Bailey, an inspiring Captain, to lead her team to an historic victory by thirteen points to five at Prairie Dunes in Kansas in 1986. The Americans, while mindful of the tightness of the match two years earlier, may have been complacent but the Great Britain & Ireland Curtis Cup girls had achieved what no other visiting side – male, female, amateur or professional – had ever done before. They had beaten the Americans on their own ground, a feat later to be matched by the European Ryder Cup side at Muirfield Village in 1987 and the Walker Cup men at Peachtree, Atlanta in 1989. The important fact is that the Curtis Cup girls did it first!

In 1988, Mrs Bailey led her team to a successful defence and although the Cup was lost in 1990, the home team won it back at Royal Liverpool in 1992 in a match which epitomized the spirit and enthusiasm of a top level transatlantic competition which all began at Wentworth.

Curtis Cup – just one of three golfing firsts as Wentworth produces champions galore

While the first Curtis Cup remains the most important amateur golf event held at Wentworth, it was only one of three landmark firsts for the Club. It staged the inaugural St Andrews Trophy in 1956 when Great Britain & Ireland beat the Continent of Europe by 10 points. Three years later, the female equivalent, the Vagliano Trophy, was also launched at Wentworth. Great Britain & Ireland won that by 12 – 3.

Wentworth has hosted two English Amateur Championships as well. In 1961, Ian Caldwell, whose international career was drawing to a close, defeated Gordon Clark, whose career was just beginning, at the 37th hole of the final. And on a baking summer's day in 1983, Craig Laurence overwhelmed Ashley Brewer by 7 and 6 after trailing early on. Brewer's performance epitomized the glorious unpredictability of golf. A 3-handicap golfer from Denham who drove with a 3-wood because he could not hit his driver, he reached the final despite the presence in the field of the English representatives from the Walker Cup team which had given such a good account of itself at Hoylake earlier in the year.

Today, Wentworth has a substantial international reputation for the quality of the World Match-play winners it highlights in the men's professional game. The Club's record, however, for producing winners of the Surrey Amateur Championship does not really stand comparison with the calibre of its victors in the Surrey Ladies'. Of course, there are some fine players among the list of men who took the Surrey title. Peter Benka was a Walker Cup player. John Davies played on four Walker Cup teams and won many prestigious amateur titles as well as being a runner-up in the Amateur Championship, the English Amateur (twice) and the Brabazon Trophy. A year after Jeremy Bennett won the Surrey title, he was the European Tour's Rookie of the Year.

The pedigree of the women winners is startling. Joyce Wethered won the Surrey Ladies' at Wentworth in the same year as that first Curtis Cup match, and other Surrey champions from Wentworth have impressive backgrounds as well. Molly Gourlay was twice English champion, Elizabeth Price won the British Ladies' Amateur in 1959, and Jill Thornhill won both those titles. All represented England on several occasions, all played in the Curtis Cup, and Mrs Thornhill was on the victorious Curtis Cup teams of 1986 and 1988. More recently, Sally Prosser won the Surrey Championship in 1986, three years after she had won the Wentworth Scratch Trophy (one of the top stroke-play events on the ladies amateur calendar) and two years before she became English Ladies' Stroke-play champion over the East course. Since turning professional, she has finished top earner on the Asian circuit. Julie Wade has been the English Under-23 champion and Anne Thompson has collected the Senior crown.

In view of something that occurred in 1951, perhaps this aspect of female ascendancy at Wentworth is rather appropriate. Remember that was the year a team of visiting American women pros beat a team of eminent male amateurs 6-0!

Talk of American women professionals takes us back to where we began – with an important international competition on the East course. Not an amateur tournament like the Curtis Cup but a professional one. The 1980 Women's British Open was won by Debbie Massey, who was to retain the title in 1981, with a six-over-par total of 294. Her path to victory was made smoother by the collapse of Marta Figueras-Dotti, then a prominent Spanish amateur, who took 6 at the last to lose by a stroke.

This was reminiscent of that first Curtis Cup and the unfortunate experience of Misses Morgan and Wethered at the eighteenth. Well that was not the only connection with the events of 1932. On hand to present the 1980 trophy to Debbie Massey was Lady Heathcoat-Amory, who before her marriage was Joyce Wethered!

No doubt she knew how poor Marta felt.

The Canada Cup

CHRIS PLUMRIDGE

For a sports-mad schoolboy growing up at the time, the 1950s represented a voyage of pure delight through some of the most memorable moments in the history of man's eternal battle to exert control over a ball. Viewed from a distance of 40 years some of these memories may have taken on a distinctly rosy hue but three of them are retained with absolute clarity. The first was the conclusion of the final Test Match at the Oval in 1953 when England regained the Ashes for the first time since the Second World War. This was the era of Len Hutton and a certain D C S Compton, everybody's boyhood hero, whose wellbeing regarding the state of his knee injury was of more national concern than the state of the economy. I can see him now, flashing the ball to the square leg boundary for what was the winning run although whether the ball actually reached the ropes is disputable since it was engulfed in a mass of exultant spectators, among whom I can count myself as a fortunate member.

The second memory comes from the same year and has its origins in the Coronation of Queen Elizabeth. With the advent of television many families obtained sets in order to view the proceedings from Westminster Abbey. In our case, there was the added incentive that if we moved quickly to buy a set we could also catch the Cup Final the month before! There was great excitement when the set arrived but when it was unveiled it was something of a disappointment. Standing about four feet tall, the burnished walnut cabinet appeared to house enough technology to send a monkey to Saturn. When the doors at the top were opened, however, they revealed a screen of such minute proportions that you had either to sit with your nose pressed against it or stand at the back of the room with a pair of strong binoculars in order to see anything.

'It looks like a tomtit sitting on a round of beef,' said Mother, always quick with the pithy comment. 'You'll have to do something.' Father, to whom these instructions were directed, made some enquiries and a few days later the solution arrived. This took the shape of a

The glittering banquet for the Canada Cup hosted by Lord Brabazon of Tara

large magnifying glass mounted on two legs which blew up the picture to viewable proportions when placed in front of the screen. When the action on the screen was confined to the centre the picture was fine but anything on the fringes became distorted by the thickness of the glass. Thus it was, we watched what I still regard as the most exciting Cup Final ever. Stanley Matthews tormented the Bolton Wanderers defence with a pair of legs which were bandy enough anyway but were even more elliptical as we watched him on a television screen which would not have been out of place in a circus hall of mirrors.

The team ethic was dominant in those days. Cricket, soccer and rugby held sway in schools and individual activities such as golf were frankly discouraged. By a fortunate accident, I arrived on this planet as the offspring of parents who not only played golf but who also had the perception to live on the edge of a golf course. Golf was, therefore, part of our daily lives and the bug had bitten deep by the time I had graduated to long trousers.

And so we come to the third memory. When it was announced that the 1956 Canada Cup would be held at Wentworth a kind of fever swept the golf fraternity. It was a fever induced by the forthcoming presence of one man, Ben Hogan, who with Sam Snead, would

Hogan was the world's best player at the time and led the winning US team. He won the individual title by five strokes

represent the United States. Aged 44 at the time, Hogan was a legend, the man who had come back from a horrific road accident and who had developed the most repeatable swing in the game. He had won the hearts and minds of the Scots in 1953 when he won the Open Championship at Carnoustie with clinical efficiency, a victory which earned him the epithet of 'the wee ice mon', and now the English were going to have the opportunity to witness his skills.

Founded in 1953 by Canadian industrialist John Jay Hopkins to promote good will through golf, the Canada Cup at Wentworth had certainly drawn a magnificent international field. Bobby Locke and a 21-year-old Gary Player were representing South Africa, Peter Thomson and Norman von Nida teamed up for Australia, Stan Leonard and Al Balding for Canada, the Miguel brothers, Sebastien and Angel, were there for Spain while the four Home Countries had Harry Weetman and Ken Bousfield for England, Harry Bradshaw and Christy O'Connor for Ireland, Eric Brown and John Panton for Scotland and Dai Rees and Dennis Smalldon for Wales.

Great names, but everyone had eyes only for Hogan. Even in practice, he and Snead were accompanied by a huge crowd watching their, or rather, *his* every move. Hogan had not played Wentworth before and wished to become familiar with every blade of grass.

If the crowds in practice had been large it was nothing compared with the gallery which gathered on the first day. In an unprecedented move it had been decided that events would start on a Sunday and thousands of people flocked to Wentworth, all with the same intention – to see Hogan. It was a lovely, sunny June day and I waited patiently with my father by the first tee for the American pair to arrive. When their turn eventually came I was mesmerized. Could this slight figure, clad in grey with the familiar white cap, really be the world's greatest golfer? There was, however, an air of detachment about him as if all that was going on around him was superfluous, and there was an intensity in his demeanour which was in stark contrast to the jovial, relaxed approach of Snead.

When Hogan struck his first drive down the fairway I sensed that not one single stroke should be missed. Because of the size of the crowd this was not possible, but by dint of some frantic running and the generosity of people who allowed me to crawl in the front, I captured most of it.

Hogan's second to the first came up a little short but then he chipped in for a 3. On the second he gained another birdie and then he was off into the country where more strokes were wrested from the card. He reached the turn in 31 and when he birdied the tenth he was, as scoring was referred to in those days, 7 under 4s.

Then, just as you were wondering how low his score might be, a hooked drive on the eleventh was followed by three putts for a 6 and the spell was broken.

The remainder of the round was steady but lacked the early

fireworks, although his 68 represented the finest round of golf I had ever seen in my young life. It was a score matched by Thomson and, with von Nida coming in with a 74, this gave Australia a two stroke lead over America and Canada. There was, however, never any doubt in my mind or anyone else's who would win.

Hogan continued in relentless fashion with rounds of 69 and 72 and Snead had improved from his first round 76 with two 73s but they still lay three strokes behind Leonard and Balding at the start of the final round. A pair of 68s from the Americans saw off the Canadian challenge and it was Locke and Player who took South Africa into the runner-up spot, a distant fourteen strokes behind the all conquering Americans. England, the leading Home Country, finished in fourth place with Wales sixth, Scotland seventh and Ireland eleventh.

No prizes for guessing who won the individual trophy: Hogan. His 277 aggregate gave him a five stroke margin over Roberto de Vicenzo with Flory van Donck in third place and Dai Rees fourth. Of passing interest, the winning team shared £773 6s 8d while Hogan pocketed £360 0s 0d for the individual prize.

The 1956 Canada Cup and the presence of Hogan had an immense impact on the game in Britain. It was the first time an international event of such magnitude had been staged here and it gave Wentworth the stature in the game which it has enjoyed since as a venue for the finest exponents and tournaments. Over thirty thousand spectators attended the three days, an unprecedented figure for those times, and it was Hogan they all wanted to see.

An original direction post, probably on the A30

(Above) A young Gary Player and Bobby Locke, the South African team, get their cards from the starter

(Left) Ben Hogan pitching from the rough at the sixteenth

87

nted
the
away
their
ountry
eonard
ns for
ointing
hey fell
hey had
m grace.

nada was
espite all
like the
is partner
emories of
hands of

ada was still
which might
not been for
ck his game
rdies. Inci-
urs and ten
ongest rounds

t was evening,
'clock, Hogan
eir opponents'

GOLF ILLUSTRATED—July 5, 1956

A RUNAWAY VICTORY

By Tom Scott

Hogan was himself—The Superb Golfer

CANADA CUP SCORES

Country	Players	1	2	3	4	Individual Total	Team Total	Total Prize
1. United States	Hogan, B.	68	69	72	68	277	567	£773 6 8
	Snead, S.	76	73	73	68	290	581	383 6 8
2. South Africa	Locke, A. D.	71	72	72	70	285	583	378 6 8
	Player, G. J.	74	73	74	76	296	586	70 0 0
3. Canada	Balding, A.	75	72	71	79	291	586	105 0 0
	Leonard, S.	69	67	71	68	295	587	
4. England	Bousfield, K.	76	71	76	73	297	589	
	Weetman, H.	76	70	76	73	297		
5. Japan	Hayashi, Y.	81	75	74	68	289		
	Ishii, M.	71	76	72	67	284		
6. Wales	Rees, D. J.	74	71	84	76	303		
	Smalldon, D.	69	74	75	69	293		
7. Scotland	Brown, E. C.	76	75	74	75	296		
	Panton, J.	72	73	73				
8. Belgium	Donck, F. V							
	Devulder, A							
9. Mexico	Clifford, P.							
	Vicenz...							
10. Australia	Nid...							

(Above) Total prize money was £2,730 in 1956. Today, any player completing the first two rounds of the Open receives £600

(Right) John Jay Hopkins, promoter of the Tournament, presenting the huge Canada Cup to the winners Ben Hogan and Sam Snead

I cannot say that watching the great man had a profound impact on my own attempts to play the game but it is enough to have the memory and to be able to say that I was there.

Perhaps the ultimate description of Hogan is best left to Pat Ward-Thomas, one of the great golf writers of the day, who wrote: 'Imagine him as he scrutinizes a long, difficult stroke, with arms quietly folded, an inscrutable quarter smile on his lips, for all the world like a gambler watching the wheel spin. And then the cigarette is tossed away, the club taken with abrupt decision, the glorious swing flashes and a long iron pierces the wind like an arrow. That was Hogan. We shall never see the like again.'

Anxious moments for commentator Henry Longhurst 'up the tower'

In the early days of televised golf, Henry Longhurst found the whole operation far more nerve-wracking than Peter Alliss does today. Covering golf at Wentworth has always been a tricky television exercise because of the layout of the course built through trees but in 1957 televised golf was even more a hit or miss affair not least for Longhurst whose commentary spot was not a warm cabin but a desk on the top of a spindly tower.

In Golf Illustrated that year, he wrote about his television experiences at Wentworth when golf was battling for late afternoon air-time on the BBC schedules, often losing out to a popular skiffle programme. When golf did manage to get air-time, getting the black and white picture on to the viewer's screen at home was quite an operation from Wentworth. Longhurst explained: 'The picture went out from a dish-shaped object on a tower to a mast at Chobham nearby and from there by air to Highgate. From there it went by land cable to Broadcasting House in the middle of London before being beamed on to Television Centre at Lime Grove in those days. Its journey was not over yet. The signal was then beamed to the transmitter at Crystal Palace then on to the viewers, including the producer at Wentworth in his scanner, the nerve centre of the operation. Don't ask me how it works,' exclaimed Longhurst.

Inside the scanner, Longhurst described the situation as controlled Babel. All the noise could be heard by him as he endeavoured, fortunately successfully, to talk eruditely and revealingly about the play. As he talked, he could hear in his ear the directions to all the cameramen who were operating like him in exposed conditions on the tops of tall towers. 'These directions were being passed on not just to the cameraman whose picture was being shown at the time and about which I was commentating but to the cameramen whose pictures would be shown next with instructions on which of the lenses on the camera should be used,' wrote Longhurst. 'In addition to all this, you hear, as commentator, the talk between the producer and your fellow commentator on another distant tower, the constant technical chatter going on between the technicians, all the telephone talk between the producer's secretary and the Lime Grove headquarters often telling her to tell you to say such-and-such when you hand over and, finally, you hear the producer's instructions to yourself which above all things you must not answer or that will go out as part of the commentary!'

The essence of golf television, wrote Longhurst, was to be up to date with the scores which were fed to him by field telephone after they had been reported to headquarters by Army signallers with walkie-talkies. The soldiers were using the golf as a field exercise.

At Wentworth in 1957 Longhurst, perched perilously at his commentary table on top of his tower, had a near disaster. Fortunately, he had a head for heights because the position from where he worked had to be reached by scaling an ordinary ladder strapped to the scaffolding. It was many years before a well-built staircase, known to this day as the Longhurst ladder, became standard. The drama did not involve his clambering up to the microphone! It happened as he tried to hold on to all his notes as the wind whistled around him.

With thankfully only five minutes to go on one of the transmission days, Longhurst recalled: 'I incautiously lifted the binoculars which were anchoring my main score sheet and, in a second, it was floating off in the wind a hundred yards away beside the ninth green.'

He survived that crisis brilliantly as you might expect of the man who set standards of television commentary few can match today.

Longhurst always felt that the commentator's role was to ensure brilliant 'flashes of silence', but having said something to that effect on air from Wentworth he ended his article by reporting: 'I received, next morning, an anonymous postcard from a gentleman in Doncaster saying simply "you open your big mouth too damn much".'

What would that viewer in Doncaster have written to some of the modern day television pundits?

More Tournaments

GORDON RICHARDSON

Tournament winners at Wentworth tend to win at Wentworth again . . . and again. Max Faulkner, Dai Rees, Henry Cotton, Bobby Locke, Peter Thomson, Christy O'Connor, Bernard Hunt, Peter Butler, Neil Coles and Malcolm Gregson all triumphed more than once at the Club – and so have Greg Norman, Seve Ballesteros, Nick Faldo and Ian Woosnam.

Abe Mitchell set the tournament victory ball rolling with his third British Match-play Championship success in 1929. It was a case of many happy returns for the dapper, tweed-jacketed man with the short backswing and powerful hands who had captained the British team which annihilated an American side led by Walter Hagen

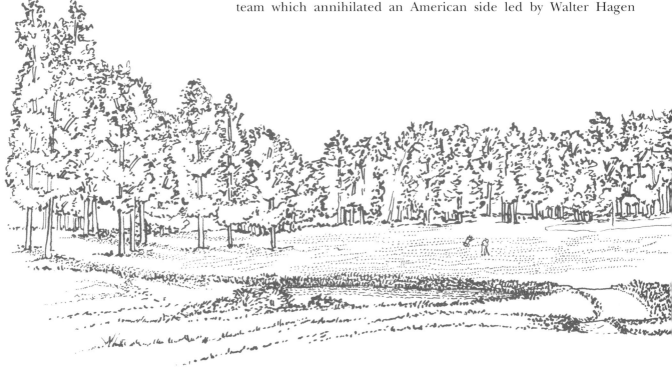

13½ – 1½ in a 'friendly' at Wentworth in 1926.

A youthful Henry Cotton, playing alongside Abe, beat Al Watrous to secure victory in the 1929 Ryder Cup match at Moortown in Leeds and seven years later – two years after the first of his three Open victories at Royal St George's – it was Cotton who became Wentworth's first stroke-play champion in the Dunlop Metropolitan event. Cotton was at the height of his powers, shooting 72, 68, 70, 71 over the mighty West course to finish three clear of Reg Whitcombe and Arthur Lacey.

Tom Scott reported in *Golf Illustrated* that the key was 'standing up to his work on the greens more like a human being and less like a praying mantis'. He added, 'Cotton, in a lean year, has probably never hit the ball better in his life and it was perfectly obvious that he had only to get on passing terms with his putter to show a clean pair of heels to his competitors'.

Astonishingly, Cotton had to wait seventeen years to complete his Wentworth double in the Dunlop 2000 Guineas tournament of 1953. It was a five round affair and Henry, by now aged 46 and on a diet to counter high blood pressure, was given little chance of success after severely rationing his tournament appearances following his 1948 Open triumph at Muirfield in Scotland. Hot favourite was reigning Open champion Bobby Locke.

Cotton, whose 65 in the third round of the 1934 Open stood as a Championship record for over 50 years and inspired Dunlop to produce their famous ball, opened his Wentworth account with another 65 and strode to a five strokes win over Dai Rees. Locke, who had an 8 at the first in round four, was another two strokes adrift.

An advertisement in Golf Illustrated *in 1926 for the Abe Mitchell – Walter Hagen Challenge match. They played much faster then with only four hours allowed for the first round and the lunch interval*

"Palakona"
£300
INVITATION
Professional
Tournament

A 36 holes Stroke Play
Tournament

will be held at the

Wentworth Golf Club
VIRGINIA WATER, SURREY
(by kind permission of the Club)

on Wednesday,
September 26th, 1934

The Tournament is organised by
Messrs. Hardy Bros., Ltd., who are
presenting the whole of the prize
money. **Every Competitor will
play with a set of Clubs shafted
with the latest "Palakona"
built Bamboo Shafts,** manufactured exclusively by Messrs. Hardy
Bros., Ltd., of Alnwick, Northumberland.

DRAW AND STARTING TIME.

STARTING TIME A.M. P.M.	Competitor's Name	STARTING TIME A.M. P.M.	Competitor's Name
10 0 2 15	ALLAN DAILEY P. P. WYNNE	10 40 2 25	JOHN ROWE W. NOLAN
10 5 2 20	MARK SEYMOUR R. S. BALLANTINE	10 45 3 0	ABE MITCHELL W. H. DAVIES
10 10 2 25	C. A. WHITCOMBE A. H. MONK	10 50 3 5	R. A. WHITCOMBE E. RAY
10 15 2 30	KEITH DALEY H. C. KINCH	10 55 3 10	A. H. PADGHAM W. T. TWINE
10 20 2 35	A. PERRY E. R. WHITCOMBE	11 0 3 15	H. P. RHODES C. S. DENNY
10 25 2 40	A. COMPSTON SYD EASTERBROOK	11 5 3 20	A. G. HAVERS W. G. OKE
10 30 2 45	GEORGE DUNCAN A. J. LACEY	11 10 3 25	HUGH ROBERTS FRED LEACH
10 35 2 50	G. PANNELL E. HOOKER	11 20 3 35	ROWLAND JONES H. KIDD PHILIP WYNNE

A Cordial Invitation is extended by Messrs. Hardy Bros. to all golfers
to attend this unique event. Admission to the Course will be free.

*A special tournament arranged by the
makers of* Palakona *bamboo shafted
clubs. A distinguished group of professionals took part and entrance for
spectators was free. Nevertheless, bamboo
shafted clubs never caught on*

Not surprisingly, there were calls for Cotton to make his comeback as playing Captain in that year's Ryder Cup back at Wentworth
but he stayed on the sidelines and Great Britain & Ireland went down
6½ – 5½.

A member of that side, and of the winning team at Lindrick four
years later, was Max Faulkner whose Wentworth double was completed in the space of three years. Faulkner, who had sailed on the
Queen Mary to make his Cup debut under skipper Cotton at Portland,
Oregon in 1947, swiftly established himself as the dandy of British golf,
lightening the postwar drabness by decking himself out in shirts, plus
twos and patent leather shoes, all of vivid hues.

This handsome son of Welsh club pro, Gustavus Faulkner, had a
colourful personality to match. Yet, it was his golf which shone
brightest over the West course when he emerged from a winter in
Monte Carlo to win the 1949 Dunlop event with a borrowed putter –
by two shots from Sam King.

A funny thing happened to Max between this victory and his
Wentworth follow-up in the 1951 Dunlop Masters – he became Open
champion! After impudently autographing a spectator's ball 'Max
Faulkner, Open champion 1951' on his way to the first tee in round
four at Royal Portrush, he proved that he had no fear of winning. He
did so again at Wentworth with a swashbuckling closing 68 to end four
shots clear of Reg Horne.

With the match-play title also to his credit that summer Max,
whose Open feat was not matched by a home player until Tony
Jacklin's 1969 success, was undeniably British golfer of the year. Golf
writers, keen to record their appreciation of what he had done, named
him Golfer of the Year. The Association of Golf Writers trophy is still
awarded annually.

Arthur Lacey (1937) and Alf Perry (1938) followed Cotton to
victory in the Dunlop Metropolitan at Wentworth. The little Australian Norman von Nida defeated stylish Belgian Flory Van Donck 6 and
5 in the final of the Star Match-play tournament in 1947. Locke, of the
looping long game and precision putting, emphasized foreign golf
power by winning the 1950 Dunlop event and 1956 Daks tournament.
Ulsterman Fred Daly restored home pride with victory in the first Daks
event in 1952. He played a starring role in the Ryder Cup at Wentworth
in 1953 by following a foursomes victory with Harry Bradshaw with a
9 and 7 thumping of Ted Kroll in the singles.

Dai Rees booked his place in the 1953 line-up against the
Americans by firing two closing 69s to win that year's Daks title but
Wentworth's own club pro Tom Haliburton came close to tieing. A
brilliant second round 65 on the East course – ten strokes better than
his opening effort on the West – was followed by a rock solid last day
141 aggregate. Only a hooked drive at the sixteenth in round four cost
the quiet spoken Scot his chance.

Like Cotton, Rees had a long wait for his second taste of success

Henry Longhurst pioneered television commentating in addition to writing for The Sunday Times

at Wentworth – nine years to be precise. At the age of 50, the bubbly Welshman triumphed by two strokes in the Dunlop Masters after a tie with Bob Charles in the Daks event to celebrate in style a week that had begun with his meeting The Queen at Buckingham Palace.

What a battler David James Rees CBE was. He beat the mighty Byron Nelson on his Ryder Cup debut in 1937, trounced Ed Furgol 7 and 6 when he skippered Great Britain & Ireland to that historic Lindrick win 20 years later and was still winning (he beat Jay Hebert and then Doug Ford in the singles) on his ninth Cup appearance, again as Captain, in 1961.

He had 40 years at the top. After a second round 66 helped him to his second Wentworth win (by two from Peter Thomson and Ralph Moffitt) he told Tom Scott 'plenty of sleep, not smoking or drinking and eating the right kind of food' was the recipe for his enduring fitness and enthusiasm both for the game and his beloved Arsenal. He was a regular visitor to Highbury.

Other 'multiple men' were legendary Irishman Christy O'Connor with victories in the 1959 Daks event, 1960 Ballantine tournament and 1964 Martini International, Bernard Hunt, winner of the 1961 Daks and 1966 Piccadilly, with a remarkable 262 tally as well as the 1960 Pickering tournament in which he partnered brother Geoff, and Peter Butler, the 1965 and 1967 Piccadilly champion. But the true Wentworth 'King' of that era was Neil Coles.

His first big Wentworth win – he closed with a record 65 and earned a record £1,500 – came in the 1961 Ballantine tournament. He finished fifth in the Order of Merit that year and, incredibly, golf's 'Mr Consistency' stayed in the top twelve for the next nineteen seasons,

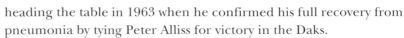

The Daks tournament was played seventeen times at Wentworth between 1952 and 1970. Winners included Fred Daly, Dai Rees (twice) Peter Alliss (twice), Bobby Locke, Peter Thomson (three times) Bob Charles and Neil Coles four times

heading the table in 1963 when he confirmed his full recovery from pneumonia by tying Peter Alliss for victory in the Daks.

He won again in 1970 at the age of 46 when he was Daks champion on his own as, indeed, he had been in 1964. I wonder what the tournament sponsors – high class men's outfitters – thought of the less than sartorial elegance of the man with the mad professor hairstyle who preferred baggy pants and floppy cardigans to natty slacks, sweaters and tailored shirts! He swung the club, however, with consummate elegance and style.

'King' Coles, who plays right-handed but does almost everything else left-handed, almost crowned his Wentworth reign by winning the first World Match-play event in his Burma Road backyard. Almost! He lost 2 and 1 in the final to Arnold Palmer.

Coles remains a Wentworth fixture, of course, as Chairman of the Board of Directors of the PGA European Tour, which has its headquarters at the Club.

Malcolm Gregson's brief love affair with the West course earned him back-to-back Daks victories and, in 1967, he topped the Order of Merit after adding the Schweppes and Martini titles. Gregson had

Jacklin 1966

Hunt 1966

Alliss 1967

Faulkner 1967

been educated at Millfield and in 1968 another former public school-boy Peter Oosterhuis, a Dulwich College product, added his name to the Wentworth roll of honour by succeeding Tony Jacklin as Viyella PGA champion in 1973.

Jacklin, who had beaten Peter into second place in 1972, wrecked his hopes of a repeat with an opening 75 after spending an hour on Wentworth's massage table trying to revive stiff and aching muscles following his participation in a two day TV 'superstars' mini-Olympics. It helped smooth the way for Oosterhuis that week as did Brian Huggett's retirement after nine holes with a pulled neck muscle – suffered while combing his hair!

Nick Job stole the show on the second day with a 63 bristling with ten birdies and an eagle which won him a car for clipping two strokes off Coles's course record, but the 6ft 5in tall Oosterhuis, whose deadly pitching and putting more than compensated for his occasionally errant long game, strode home. He was European number one four years running and headed for the US Tour in 1975 with a record of having won 20 of the 200 events he played this side of the Atlantic. In that time, he had 26 seconds, seventeen thirds and 116 top tens, yet

Oosterhuis (centre) with Dudley Millensted

Gallacher 1970

Coles 1970

would win only once in the States when taking the Canadian Open on the US Tour in 1981. Midlander Maurice Bembride, who had knocked out Oosterhuis with a 65 to a 70 in that year's Piccadilly Medal final, beat him into second place again in the 1974 Viyella event, birdieing the last four holes on the West course to storm from six behind to win. His closing 64 matched his record 64 that year in the US Masters.

Two men set to dominate the next golfing era, Greg Norman (1979 and 1981) and Severiano Ballesteros (1980), monopolized the Martini International at Wentworth. Australia's Norman triumphed in wet and wintry weather in 1979 with a strict par 288 in a weird week which saw former Liverpool maths master John Morgan run him close, Jacklin return two 77s, Coles miss a 1inch putt, and Brian Barnes hurl a tee box into a nearby garden at the fourth tee after being penalized two strokes for being six minutes late for his start.

When the PGA Championship, sponsored from 1984 to 1987 by Whyte and Mackay, returned to make its permanent home at Wentworth, Yorkshire's Howard Clark emerged the first winner in an event reduced to three rounds because of heavy rain. Kent's Paul Way succeeded him, closing with a 66 to tie Wentworth resident Sandy Lyle, triumphing at the third extra hole after Sandy had fluffed a four-foot winner on the previous green. Way hit two great shots to that third extra hole – the par 5 seventeenth. The ball finished through the green and that power play confirmed his star status. He was English Stroke-play champion and a Walker Cup international at eighteen, Dutch Open champion after a closing 65 in his rookie pro season at nineteen and a key figure on his Ryder Cup debut a year later in 1983 – when he was partnered by Seve Ballesteros – an inspired move by Captain Tony Jacklin.

Yet it is Bernhard Langer's 1987 PGA victory they still talk about at Wentworth. Despite vile weather over the first two days, the German's record eighteen-under-par 270 aggregate was four strokes better than that of arch rival Ballesteros in second place and eleven better than Australian Rodger Davis's winning score in 1986.

'No one could have beaten Bernhard this week – his four rounds were unbelievable,' said Seve whose own score was twelve strokes better than his 1980 winning total in the Martini event. Six years later, in 1993, Langer would triumph again almost as impressively.

Ian Woosnam, who had suffered a rotten start to the year after winning eight tournaments and £1 million in 1987, bounced back to beat Ballesteros and Mark James with a 274 score in 1988 and in 1989, Wentworth member Nick Faldo, fresh from his US Masters triumph, finally got his name on the Club's winners roster, a sixteen-under-par score edging him two ahead of Ryder Cup partner Woosnam. He went on to complete a 'spring double' in the Dunhill British Masters a week later, added the French Open crown, then returned to complete a West course same year double over Woosnam in the Suntory World Match-play event.

Bernhard Langer, twice a PGA Championship winner round the West course. He set the Championship record of eighteen-under-par in 1987

Faldo was a hard act to follow but, amazingly, Ballesteros stole his thunder when he, too, did the Wentworth double in 1991, ending fourteen months without a European Tour win. He took the Volvo PGA title with a typical flourish at the first extra hole. He hit a classic 200-yard 5-iron to 3 feet for a winning birdie after a tie at seventeen-under-par with Colin Montgomerie.

'Many people were thinking that Seve would not come back – today I proved them wrong,' declared the Spaniard who went on to equal Gary Player's five World Match-play title wins and top the Volvo Order of Merit for a record sixth time.

For Seve with seven Wentworth wins to his credit it was a case of move over 'King' Coles! Now Seve rules the Burma Road!

Seve Ballesteros playing in the Martini International (May 1979) at Wentworth

World Match-play
Player sets the pace

BOB FERRIER

Memory can be a fickle friend but some memories abide. The most abiding memory I have of the World Match-play Championship is of a fellow named Philip Wilson and me standing behind the first tee as Arnold Palmer struck the first shot of the first match in the first round of the first event on a misty October morning in 1964, and saying almost with one voice, 'It can't be true'. Yet true it was and the Piccadilly, as it came to be called and as many people still think of it, went on to become one of the most remarkable, most successful, commercially sponsored events the sport has known.

That distant October day was the culmination of two years of plotting and planning and hard work. Carreras Rothmans, the tobacco company which staged the event, was already involved in golf with the Piccadilly tournament at Hillside, which was won by five times Open champion Peter Thomson of Australia. It featured the first ever

£2,000 first prize and a total of £8,000, bettered only by the Open Championship. The Carreras people thought it a success but wanted something different from the routine 72 hole stroke-play tournament which all the other sponsors ran.

I first met Mark McCormack when I was wearing my journalist's hat on a trip to the US Masters. When he came to London to explore UK commercial opportunities for his clients – Arnold Palmer, Gary Player and Jack Nicklaus at that time – he used my office and told me of his conception of a World Match-play Championship which he had almost 'sold' to a Japanese company. He was to do just that fifteen years later! The idea was that the best eight players in the world, based on their current achievements and career histories, would be invited to play a match-play competition – 36 holes and when you lost you went home. Because only eight players would be involved the sponsor could treat them particularly grandly, providing special treatment for wives who were seen as being very important in McCormack's thinking, exceptional accommodations, private limousines and so on. Ideally, it would be in the London area.

I had been retained by Carreras as a consultant and quickly wheeled in Mark to meet the aforementioned Philip Wilson, now deceased, Michael Lock and George Hammond. Wilson was Director of Advertising, Lock was Director of Public Relations and Hammond was one of his top lieutenants. George Hammond would become a major personality in the management of the event. He still acts as official starter today.

It has to be appreciated that Carreras Rothmans, like other cigarette companies at that time, was awash with money to spend on promotions. Cigarettes are an ultimate consumer product like bread – bought today, used today, bought again tomorrow. These companies may not have a licence to print money but cash flow is seldom a problem. McCormack took care not to 'guarantee' the presence of his

Neil Coles played in the first World Match-play and reached the final. No other British player would do that until 1980 and no Briton would win until Ian Woosnam in 1987

clients, merely indicating that he was sure they would be interested. First prize was to be £5,000 with a total of £16,000. McCormack quickly got a 'yes' to his proposal.

Television coverage would be critical. We met Brian Cowgill, then head of sport at the BBC. Despite the difficulties of covering match-play – you never know at which hole a match will finish – Cowgill was an immediate enthusiast.

Next, we had to find a golf course. It should be in the London area not only because of the obvious Piccadilly association but because London golf fans seldom had a chance to see the world's best in the flesh. With its experience of the Ryder Cup and the Canada (now World) Cup in the 1950s, Wentworth was clearly the place.

All the pieces fell together. The cast assembled. Arnold Palmer was US Masters champion, Ken Venturi, US Open champion, Tony Lema, Open champion, winning on his very first visit to the Old course at St Andrews. Jack Nicklaus was Canada Cup individual winner, Gary Player, Australian Open champion, Bruce Devlin held the New Zealand Open title. Neil Coles had won the British Match-play, Peter Butler, who had played with distinction in the US Masters and the Carling World Championship, was his runner-up. So the game was on.

Why Mark McCormack always knew he was on to a good thing

Many times I have been asked what were my thoughts behind the creation of the World Match-play Championship. The Championship has become one of the most prominent fixtures on the world golf calendar, having continued from 1964 with the support of Piccadilly (1964-76) and three subsequent sponsors – Colgate (1977-78), Suntory (1979-90) and Toyota, the current sponsor, from 1991.

Match-play is the way the game began and it is the form of golf that the average player enjoys when he goes out with friends on the weekend. I felt that a tremendous void was created when the PGA Championship in America was switched from match – to stroke-play in 1958. There was another match-play event in Britain at the time, but it did not have an international field and certainly lacked the greats in the world of golf.

Staged on the famed West course at the Wentworth Club, the World Match-play Championship would become an autumn tradition. There were eight players in the original field whereas today there are twelve. I think twelve is the ideal number; eight is too few and sixteen is too many.

Match-play – knockout – was considered preferable to round robin, which, while it may be popular, good promotion, and attractive for television, is not pure golf. The matches were to be 36 holes because anybody can beat anybody over eighteen holes while over 36 holes the better player is much more likely to win.

It was stressed that it was absolutely essential for the invitation system to be flexible since there would be times when Arnold Palmer – or whoever ought to be in the field by virtue of being one of the top players in the world – could not qualify because he had not won a tournament in a firmly established system. It was ultimately decided to invite the winners of the US Masters, US Open and British Open and subsequently, the defending champion of the new undertaking.

Initially, the British PGA put pressure on the sponsors to include the top player in its Order of Merit. However, it was felt there was no reason to include a British player in the field if he did not warrant selection as a player of world class. Neil Coles was selected early

Vast crowds poured into Wentworth. The estate was overrun. Cars were parked on driveways, roads, verges. Even the milkmen could not get through to deliver. Residents were up in arms. As the traffic piled up on the A30 several miles back down to Egham, the police were less than best pleased. They were seriously overstretched. The second year, 1965, was not much better but eventually huge car parks were created to take the bulk of the influx.

A generation or more on, it is difficult for contemporary golfers who properly have their idols in Ballesteros and Faldo to comprehend what Arnold Palmer meant to golf in the 1960s. In America he was – there is no other description for it – a folk hero. When he won that first World Match-play he put a mark of distinction on the event which it has never lost in good days and bad.

For the first few years, players and wives were put up at the Carlton Tower in Sloane Street, the right side of town for the drive to Wentworth. Later it was felt that it was just another big city hotel which lacked an 'English' flavour. So what better than River Suites at The Savoy with living rooms as big as tennis courts, bathrooms not much smaller, stunning views over the river and every service imaginable? No sooner said than done!

on but there was one year when no British player was asked and this created a great many problems. But there was none who deserved to be selected, and staging a golf tournament in Britain without a British player was a necessary gamble.

How times were to change. British and European players came to dominate golf worldwide. From Palmer, Player and Jack Nicklaus in the early years to Seve Ballesteros, Greg Norman, Ian Woosnam, Sandy Lyle and Nick Faldo in more recent times, the World Match-play Championship has been ruled by the leading golfers of each successive era.

I dare say that no event has had a more impressive roster of champions. With two notable exceptions – Graham Marsh and Isao Aoki – every winner of the World Match-play Championship has also won a title in one of the four traditional major championships.

The event has been described as a 'small miracle' and by Gary Player as 'the fifth most important golf tournament in the world'. After winning the 1992 Championship, Nick Faldo observed: 'What does this event mean to me? Well, it has been going for 30 years and all the great players have competed in it and won.

It does capture the interest and it is a unique event. It is a real championship – 36 holes each day on this course in autumn is a physical and mental challenge.'

There have been many great matches over the years – Player against Tony Lema, Tony Jacklin versus Lee Trevino, and Sandy Lyle's comeback against Faldo, to name but three. The choice of Wentworth as the venue has been good for the Championship. There is no question that the event has been good for the Club.

Gary Player versus Tony Lema, 1965

It was, said Gary Player, the most fantastic head-to-head match he had ever played. One up after nine holes, Player was six down after eighteen, seven down after nineteen, five down with nine to play and all square at the 36th. 'The match,' Player said, 'contains my whole life story.'

Twelve months earlier on the same course in the same event in the same round, he had been thrashed 8 and 6 by Arnold Palmer. It made Player aware that his nerves were shot and he set about a course of recovery which included body building exercises with Mr Universe. When Player revisited Wentworth he was the US Open champion, having beaten Jack Nicklaus to a Grand Slam.

In the eight man field, Player beat Neil Coles and Lema put out Peter Alliss. As far as Player was concerned, there was spice to the semifinal. Lema had been critical of the 'Big Three' – Player, Palmer and Nicklaus – and had signed with Slazenger who had dropped Player.

From the tenth hole in the morning Lema won seven holes in a row and had six birdies. Coming off the seventeenth green. Lema started to talk.

'He did not say I had no chance, 'Player recalled, 'but I got the impression he was thinking it. At that moment I knew I was going to win.'

If the Lema camp put the champagne on ice, Player had a quick lunch and went to the practice ground. He lost the nineteenth and some of the gallery started to leave, missing the recovery that began when Player won the next two holes with birdies and the fifth.

'I thought of Lema all the time . . . my strategy was to keep gnawing at him,' said Player. At the sixth hole Player heard a spectator write him off and sharply retorted: 'A match is never won until the last putt has been holed so stick around and you might see something that will surprise you.'

On the sixth green Player missed a two-foot putt but while walking to the seventh he said he had a spiritual experience. He felt suddenly 'drenched in adrenaline'.

At the turn in the afternoon round he was still five down but won the tenth and eleventh. He also won the thirteenth with a 3 after Lema had holed from 25 feet. Two down with three to play, Player hit a big drive on the sixteenth and Lema hooked a 3-wood into the trees. One down with two to play!

At the seventeenth Lema holed from 12 feet for a birdie 4 and Player, to keep the match alive, got down from 7 feet. One down, one to play.

Player won the eighteenth, the 36th, of the match with a 3-wood approach that finished 20 feet from the hole. The crowd was delirious but Player admitted: 'When I hit the ball I thought it was an awful shot. I came off it but it went through the trees.'

At the first play-off hole, Lema hooked his approach into a bunker and Player won with a 4 to a 5. For the first time that day Player began to tremble uncontrollably. He sat by the edge of the green and lost consciousness for a few seconds. 'The manner in which Tony Lema took his appalling defeat,' Player said, 'was simply outstanding.'

TIM GLOVER

Likeable Lema, who happily dispensed largesse to the Press, won his Open after only one practice round. He was killed in a flying accident in 1966

The drive from The Savoy through London traffic, however, became too much. A helicopter service from Battersea was offered but only Palmer and Peter Thomson used it. Eventually, the travel problem was solved simply by renting a house for each player and his entourage on the Wentworth estate or in the Ascot area.

Above all else, however, it has been the play and the players that have made it such an outstanding event. The very distinctive character of the World Match-play brought the great stars of the day to Wentworth – the 'Big Three', of course, but also Lee Trevino, Billy Casper, Tony Jacklin, Peter Thomson, Tony Lema, Roberto de Vicenzo, Bob Charles, Gene Littler, Ken Venturi, Tommy Aaron, many of whom remained tremendously loyal to the event. Over the years, they produced marvellous matches and outstanding public entertainment.

In 1965 there was the classic Lema-Player semi-final which will be talked about as long as the old game is played, with Player coming back from five down with nine regulation holes to play to win at the 37th. What was largely overlooked that year was the other semi-final, quite different in character, between Palmer and Thomson who had had to play 37 holes in the first round to beat influenza victim Christy O'Connor. Here were two of golf's most successful, most experienced and most determined players face to face and competing with marvellous intensity, giving and taking no quarter until, at last, Thomson birdied the final hole to win.

In 1966, the first day produced two remarkable first eighteen hole efforts – Palmer was round in 66 to be five up on De Vicenzo, and Nicklaus breezed round in 64 to be five up on Dave Thomas. Player,

The vast crowd on the fourth fairway following the Gary Player-Peter Thomson final in 1965 which Player won

Extrovert Lee Trevino, who lost the final in 1970, annoyed Tony Jacklin with his chatter two years later

who was defending the title that year, beat Neil Coles and Palmer on successive days and beat Nicklaus 6 and 4 in a final that is remembered for the incident Nicklaus had with the referee Tony Duncan.

In 1967, Gay Brewer, the US Masters champion, was critical of the 'Big Three', saying there were lots of better players. Drawn against him in a first round match, Gary Player, one of the 'Three' and never a man to miss a chance with the writers, declared: 'I will let my clubs do the talking.'

The match, silent and tense, went to extra holes. At the 39th, Brewer drove to the left side of the fairway. Noticing that the green-keeper had already cut a new hole for the next day's play on the right of the green, Brewer insisted that this was wrong and that they should play to the original hole. After much discussion with the referee Michael Bonallack, now Secretary of the Royal & Ancient Golf Club of St Andrews, this was done. Brewer promptly lost the hole. Not one word was spoken in the limousine that took them back to the club-house.

In 1968, Tony Jacklin appeared on the scene for the first time. Helped by a putter he had unearthed in a dark corner of Tom Weiskopf's home in Ohio several weeks earlier, Jacklin quickly disposed of Lee Trevino to line up a match with Player in the semi-final.

Once again, 36 holes, much of it played in a downpour which

Jack Nicklaus versus Lee Trevino, 1970

Lee Trevino had never won in Britain. Jack Nicklaus had never won the World Match-play. One American's dream would be realized. Trevino was round in the morning in 69 and was three down but lunch was an appetizer to a brilliant display of golf in the afternoon.

Supermex birdied the first, the fourth and the ninth but still found himself five down at the turn. The seventh typified Trevino's misfortune. Nicklaus had a blind second shot in the right rough which would have flown the green but for hitting a spectator on the shoulder. His ball rebounded to within a yard of the flag and, after kissing the helpful shoulder, the Golden Bear rolled in the putt to win the hole. Trevino needed a shoulder to cry on!

Nicklaus went out in 32 but he did not have such a comfortable journey coming home. Trevino set the gallery alight, winning four out of five holes from the tenth. The twelfth was halved in birdies. Nicklaus, his

lead cut to one hole, then played one of the shots of the week to the fifteenth green, a 4-iron that got inside Trevino's ball. When he holed the putt for a birdie, Nicklaus was two up with three to play.

Again Trevino came back, winning the sixteenth with a birdie, his fifth in eight holes. Once again the seventeenth, the longest hole on the course, would entice triumph and disaster. Because the fairway slopes dramatically left to right, the temptation is to drive left of centre and allow gravity to do the rest. Trevino, who throughout the Championship had played the hole with a slight hook into the high side of the slope, overdid it this time and his ball took one bounce and shot towards the fence bordering the gardens on the left. Trevino waited on the tee until he saw the signal he was dreading – a wave of the arms from an official to indicate that the ball was out of bounds.

Nicklaus selected a 1-iron and a few minutes later they shook hands. Jack had won his only World Match-play title.

TIM GLOVER

Jacklin versus Trevino, 1972

Lee Trevino's constant chattering over the years has made him a popular figure with the galleries but not always with his opponents and certainly not always with Tony Jacklin! When they met in the 1972 World Match play Championship, Jacklin made it plain he did not care for what Mark McCormack called 'Trevino's tension relieving banter' in his report of the encounter in The World of Professional Golf.

Trevino responded by telling Jacklin that he did not have to listen. Jacklin took his advice on the front nine in the afternoon when he turned a four hole lunch time deficit into a one hole advantage. This was the second time they had met. Jacklin had won an earlier, far less dramatic Wentworth duel comfortably enough but the 1972 duel would be a classic.

At lunchtime, Jacklin was angry. He felt that he had allowed Trevino to talk him out of it. He was self-critical of the way he had handled himself in the morning. 'I've been a bloody fool,' he said. In the afternoon he stayed out of earshot of Trevino, played some of the best golf of his career and in the end still lost to a player whose game was equally brilliant.

The fans loved it. There was so much tension and excitement in the air you could have cut it with a knife as Jacklin clawed his way back. An eagle at the fourth, birdies at the next two and he was only one down. A 6-iron to 1 foot at the eighth squared the match. A 3 at the ninth where he hit a 5-iron to 6 feet saw him out in 29 and one up. Great stuff!

Jacklin's 1-iron tee shot at the tenth ended up, however, in the folds of a lady's skirt as she sat beside the green. The ball reappeared when she stood up but the incident broke Jacklin's well focused concentration. He parred but Trevino made 2!

They had caught up by now with the Weiskopf-Oosterhuis semi-final ahead of them. Waiting to play their shots just added to the tension. One by one the holes were halved coming home, Jacklin sinking a putt of 5 feet at the fifteenth, Trevino from 4 feet. At the seventeenth, Jacklin hit the stick with his approach. Coming down the last, the match was still square.

It was then that Trevino hit a classic winner. With Jacklin having missed the green with his second, the American pulled out a 3-wood and smashed the ball 230 yards to within 9 feet of the stick – the shot of a champion. His closing birdie gave him victory.

Wrote promoter McCormack: 'What will make the Trevino-Jacklin match live forever in the memories of all those fortunate enough to see it, was the fact that both men played so superbly.'

BILL ELLIOT

flooded some greens, were not enough to reach a decision. The light was not good enough and the course was arguably unplayable so the players could not complete the match that day. Nor, in fact, the next day.

Finally on the Sunday, 38 hours after they had played the 36th hole, Jacklin and Player went back out to continue the match. It took just over ten minutes for Player, who had by now put his stamp on the Championship, to beat Jacklin and win the right to take on left-hander Bob Charles in the final.

Even that early in the morning the crowds were again huge. Jacklin hit the green in two. Player missed the green and was 9 feet away in three shots. As Jacklin went to putt he was dazzled by the sun shining on a young boy's periscope. He asked the boy to move, then dragged the putt 4 feet wide and short of the hole. Now Player stepped forward. He interrupted his procedure to ask photographers to move and to request that the crowd, whom he suggested were against him, give him the courtesy of letting him putt. Some reports said there had been more than a suggestion that someone had whispered 'miss it, miss it' when he had originally been over the ball!

In the end he holed and Jacklin missed. Another chapter in the tense head to head history of the World Match-play had been written.

Player went on to beat New Zealander Bob Charles that year by a hole but the following year he trounced Jean Garaialde of France 10 and 8 in a first round match. If it looked to be shaping up to a repeat of the 1968 final, American Gene Littler had other ideas and reeled off seven successive 3s from the fifth against Player. It was Littler whom Charles met in the final and it was Charles who won with as devastating a performance of putting from all angles and ranges as has been seen at Wentworth.

In 1970, when proudly holding the US Open title, Jacklin gained revenge over Player but did not make the final. That year, it was

Gary Player versus Hale Irwin, 1974

Pressure stalks its prey wearing different cloaks. There is the faltering that comes when a golfer simply funks a match, realizing that the target is beyond him. Then there is the shaking that begins as an opponent turns the screw and an adrenalin surge suddenly becomes mixed up with nerve gas. Worst of all, there is the pressure that is applied when a great player realizes a part of his game is disintegrating before his horrified gaze.

This was exactly the scenario when Gary Player played Hale Irwin. It was Player's sixth final. On the previous five occasions the South African reached the final, he had won, the only man to have competed in every World Match-play Championship since it began in 1964.

Hardly surprising then that he was the overwhelming favourite to win a sixth title when he took on the tall, slim, bespectacled American. Not that anyone underestimated Irwin. Hale was good, very good, but Player was recognized as the greatest match-player on earth. This final was to be, if not a stroll, then a march to victory for the little man.

Player had spent his professional life, however, fighting a hook off the tee. He feared the surfacing of this hook like other men fear more obvious beasts. He

had even visited Ben Hogan to seek the great man's views on how to cure the fault and he arrived at Wentworth believing he had found the secret.

So when Player hooked his opening drive behind a bush the significance was immense. He lost the hole to a typically solid par by Irwin but it was the birth of self-doubt that was crucial even at this early stage.

Another hooked drive off the third tee cost Player a second hole. Typically, this most pugnacious of golfers pulled himself together and even edged one hole ahead of Irwin only to hit his worst hook of the day at the ninth. His anger with his own inadequacy at this point was fearsome.

If Player could have hit himself he would have done so. By now, Irwin was almost an irrelevance. Restrained and cool, he was Mr Par brought to life. Meanwhile, Player was becoming a fidgeting wreck, especially when he missed an 18 inch putt on the eleventh green!

Now, if the hook was Player's cross, then the short, missed putt was both hammer and nails to him. Suddenly, he knew this round on a course he adored could turn into all his worst nightmares rolled into one jumbo nightmare.

Still, he managed to maintain a one hole lead by the end of the morning round and his battalion of fans lunched more confident than the player that their hero would sort himself out.

It was not to be. Player hooked more shots and

Trevino against Nicklaus with the Golden Bear, five up with nine to play, winning by 2 and 1.

Trevino, in the days when his back could stand up to two rounds a day, lost the final to Tom Weiskopf two years later in 1972, a year memorable in World Match-play history for the match between him and Jacklin. The British player, who earlier in the year had traumatically lost the Open to Trevino at Muirfield when the American had chipped in to win the 71st hole, was four down at lunch but covered the front nine in 29 in the afternoon to go one up. The match went all the way before Trevino triumphed.

Over the years the Piccadilly World Match-play Championship became something more than just another golf tournament. It was a marvellous climax to the golfing season and increasingly a social event. And those few of us left who were in at the beginning feel enriched by it all.

continued to putt badly. Irwin, encouraged by this and playing ever more steadily as his opponent ranted and raved at himself, moved one up with five to play.

Irwin completed this hole in a safe par. Player then just missed his fifteen-foot birdie putt and the crowd began to move on as the referee announced that the hole had been halved in 4. Not as far as Irwin was concerned. He raised his eyebrow a fraction. Player sighed, stepped forward, tapped his ball towards the cup and then watched incredulously as his ball rimmed the hole and stayed out.

At that instant Player imploded, his muscular body sagging like an old deck chair. The pressure had got to him as never before. He had not lost yet but he had assuredly just beaten himself. Though he halved the following three holes, Player duly conceded when he missed another short putt on the next.

He was a gracious loser but his eyes blazing with indignation gave the game away. When the big moments had arrived that day Player had missed them and he hated himself for it. He would never make a World Match-play final again.

BILL ELLIOT

Hale Irwin, winner by 3 and 1 over Gary Player in 1974, hits his tee shot at the fourteenth

The 'Nicklaus Incident' makes headlines 1966

Jack Nicklaus was rightly named America's Golfer of the Century. He might legitimately claim to be the greatest golfer who ever lived although comparisons between different eras are always difficult. There is no doubting his magnificent contribution to the game over a sustained period of time, of his impressive competitive record, and of the marvellous legacy of new courses he has building or has built around the world. For over 30 years he and his delightful wife Barbara have graced the international golfing scene.

He has been an inspiration to millions. He has prompted many of today's stars to consider golf as a career. Nick Faldo caught the golfing bug watching Nicklaus on television playing at Augusta where Faldo has so far won two Green Jackets. Nicklaus has six.

The Golden Bear, a nickname first coined for him in Australia, has won five US PGA Championships, four US Opens and three British Opens. His majors record may never be broken. Only four players have ever won all four annual majors of world golf at least once. Nicklaus has done it three times.

He is a golfing god yet, in 1966, months after winning his first Open at Muirfield, he was involved in a bizarre incident at Wentworth. It involved a confrontation on course between Nicklaus and respected amateur official Colonel Tony Duncan. World Match-play sponsors Piccadilly had invited Duncan to act as referee of the Jack Nicklaus – Gary Player final.

Incredibly, Nicklaus got so riled by Duncan's failure to give him the ruling he felt he deserved in the rough at the ninth that he went to the length of accepting Duncan's offer, one hole later, to stand down as referee and wrote to him three weeks later about it. Even more curiously, he indicated in his note that he would give a copy of the note to the newspapers. This sad incident is still very much alive in Colonel Duncan's mind but in 1993 Nicklaus, contacted during the US Masters at Augusta, had little to add to a subject he has long forgotten and would prefer others to forget as well. Rumours that his view had softened towards Duncan

Tony Duncan, the match referee explains the ruling which Jack Nicklaus objected to in the 1966 World Match-play Final. Duncan later withdrew and Gerald Micklem took over

proved unfounded.

'What do you want me to do?' he asked when tackled, 'Make a rebuttal?' Nicklaus insists that the issue is now well and truly dead and should be firmly laid to rest. Twenty-seven years on, Jack Nicklaus still thinks he was right.

Colonel Duncan, a former Walker Cup Captain and a member of the Royal & Ancient Golf Club of St Andrews, had refereed the first two finals. He recalls the unfortunate occasion with total clarity. He makes the salient point that what made the incident so bizarre is the fact that, to his knowledge, Nicklaus has behaved impeccably on the course ever since. He might, as an example, have mentioned Nicklaus's magnificent sporting gesture to Tony Jacklin three years later when he conceded Tony's missable final putt in the 1969 Ryder Cup at Royal Birkdale which enabled Great Britain & Ireland to draw the match against the Americans. Yet in 1966 Nicklaus, it seemed, was ready to stand up for what he thought were his rights even if it meant taking on officialdom.

Colonel Duncan will never forget the incident. This is how he remembers that day:

'After a quiet start, Player was one up after eight holes. At the ninth, Nicklaus hit an enormous hook off the tee. The ball finished in the ditch guarding the out-of-bounds fence. Nicklaus asked what he could do and I said he could drop under one stroke penalty two club lengths from the ditch which, at his request, I marked out. He reluctantly dropped into thickish heather.

On addressing the ball, he espied a Piccadilly advertisement sign about sixty yards ahead and slightly to the left of his direct line to the pin. Under the local line of sight rule used for this tournament, he requested a further drop. I stood behind his ball and saw that the advertisement sign was not directly in line with the ball and the pin. I therefore declined his request.'

Whether it was, as Nicklaus suggested later, Colonel Duncan's parade ground manner that threw him off or, indeed, his own stubborness, he does admit that he should have handled the situation better, certainly the public relations aspects of it, as he explains in the book he wrote with Herbert Warren Wind entitled The Greatest Game of All.

Colonel Duncan declined to referee again.

Gary Player won the final.

Jack Nicklaus whose conduct and deportment on the course has been impeccable. What happened at Wentworth was an isolated incident

World Match-play
Norman and Seve

DAVID DAVIES

|f any two men can seriously be said to have swashbuckled their way through golf in the 1970s and 1980s, to have played the game as if with sabre and musket, it is the two men who dominated the World Match-play Championship throughout the period 1977-86, Severiano Ballesteros and Greg Norman. It is, of course, no surprise that these two men were so successful in this particular event. Both thrive on the format. For each, the chance to look into an opponent's eyes, and say without speaking, 'do you really think you can beat me?' is a moment to be relished.

Each is an imperious man. Each strides on to the first tee to attend to the formalities. Other than that, neither man pays much attention to his opponent. He is there only to be dismissed. The demeanour of each suggests that neither anticipates any problem, that this is only a little local difficulty. Both play their golf with bravado, with extravagant flourishes and strike at stricken opponents with the glee of a boarding party of pirates who have blown the opposing vessel to smithereens. Seve is the one with the black eyepatch, Greg wears the bandana.

All this, of course, makes them hugely exciting to watch as well as supremely successful. In the period in question, the Spaniard played four finals, winning them all, and the Australian won his three finals. They did not, more is the pity, ever play each other in a final although they did meet twice in earlier rounds.

In 1981, Ballesteros was having one of those weeks when no one else need turn up. He beat American Hale Irwin 6 and 4 in the first round. Norman was summarily dispatched by 8 and 6, and went on to beat Germany's Bernhard Langer 5 and 4. In the final he beat Ben Crenshaw by one hole. Norman avenged himself two years later, winning by one hole in the semi-final. It is perhaps appropriate that, for the moment, there is parity between the two men.

Alike in their attitudes as Ballesteros and Norman are, they could hardly be more different in appearance. Seve is all saturnine, a dark-haired, brooding presence but whose face can change instantly, totally illuminated by a devastating smile. He dresses in dark colours with the Spanish taste for subdued hues, frequently wearing navy blue, his lucky colour. Greg, taller, broader-shouldered, waspier-waisted, has a mane of blond hair frequently topped by a white fedora, and his clothes reflect the bright, white heat of his birthplace, Queensland. A smile is never far from Norman's face; he grins as he bites 'yer legs'.

Ballesteros, of course, is the senior man. Just as in the period being covered he won four times in the Match-play to Norman's three, by 1992 he had won five majors to the Australian's one. He is one of the game's all-time great talents, while Norman has the potential to be one of the game's great players. One title and three losing play-offs in major championships is not an adequate return on Norman's ability.

Ballesteros won in 1981, 1982, 1984 and 1985; Norman in 1980, 1983 and 1986, a dominance of the kind that Arnold Palmer, Gary Player and Jack Nicklaus used to inflict on the US Masters. Just as those three revitalized championship golf in America in the late 1950s and

For seven years Greg (left) and Seve stole the show!

1960s, so the Seve 'n' Greg Show would fill Wentworth a decade or two later. Those of us who were there to see it know how fortunate we were.

Norman was the first to win, beating Sandy Lyle in 1980. That had not looked very likely in the second round when he was four down to Nick Faldo. However, Faldo was rather more fallible then than later in the decade and Norman won at the 38th. The Australian was keen to

Sandy Lyle versus Nick Faldo, 1982

This duel between British golf's young lions was eagerly anticipated. The easy-going Scot against the cool, calculating Englishman was a promoter's dream. Some newspapers, indeed, referred to the match in boxing terms, calling it a clash of heavyweights, perhaps even of future world champions. How right they were.

Lyle and Faldo have always been serious rivals. Each has judged himself against the other throughout careers that have been locked together since their amateur days when Lyle indisputably held the edge.

Both would go on to win World Match-play titles along with so many other big events but on this day in 1982 it was naked pride that was at stake. By lunch the pride was expanding in one chest more than in the other. Faldo was six holes up. Lyle was reeling, his confidence flailed by a back nine onslaught from Nick. Faldo had come home in 33, four-under-par. With Lyle struggling on the greens that was good enough to win Faldo four holes and make Lyle believe – for a moment only – that the match was all but over.

'I just determined to go out in the afternoon and give it a rip. I did not want him to win 9 and 8. I expected defeat but I wanted at least respectability,' he later admitted. Something significant happened, however, before Lyle went out to give it a rip. He changed putters from a heavy blade to a softer, centre shafted model. The greens were too fast for the blade. The ball was coming off the face too fast and that was what had really done the damage in the morning.

It was an inspired move. Lyle holed a tricky four-footer for a half at the first hole and the confidence began to pump back into him. An eight-foot birdie at the short second brought a smile at last and he positively beamed after Faldo messed up the third to give him another win.

A long birdie putt at the fourth won another hole and the deficit was cut to three holes. Still, Faldo could not really lose, could he? Oh yes he could. By the turn, he was just one hole ahead of Lyle, the victim of his own mistakes and Sandy's inspired putting. By now paying customers were sprinting from all over the course, deserting the other matches to focus on the main event.

Even now, however, Lyle was still not thinking of winning. He had achieved his objective and he determined to stay relaxed and to carry on ripping. They were good tactics. Faldo, so in control during the morning, was beginning to fray visibly at the edges as more holes were lost.

He was rattled and it showed. It was understandable. By the thirteenth, the prospect of a stunning victory finally entered Lyle's head as he holed a five-foot birdie putt to move one up. This became two up at the fifteenth where Faldo hit into a bunker and bogeyed. The sixteenth was halved. The seventeenth and the match went to Lyle after Faldo made a hash of his drive and Sandy holed from 27 feet for birdie, a closing putt that summed up his glorious afternoon but a putt that struck Faldo like a knife twisting in the gut.

Really, you had to be there. Those of us who were there will always remember it. So, too, will Lyle. 'I didn't expect to win all those holes and I'm sure he didn't expect to lose them. It's unbelievable what can happen in match-play. It often happens at Wentworth and it happened today,' he reflected.

Most observers considered this to be something of an understatement.

BILL ELLIOTT

beat Lyle having finished second the previous week, a single stroke behind him in the Dunlop Masters. He lost out to Lyle, too, by a mere £278 at the top of the Order of Merit. It was close. The way they played the last hole of the match, the 36th, where they were all square, demonstrated Lyle's lack of aggression at that time. Norman smashed a driver almost three hundred yards down the fairway. Lyle took the 1-iron for safety and could not match Norman's birdie. The title and the £14,000 that the Australian won made up for the previous week's disappointment.

Ballesteros was to win in 1981, a less than vintage year overall, although for a Spaniard to beat an American, Ben Crenshaw in this case, still carried an element of surprise about it. Ballesteros had 20 birdies in his first two rounds but the final was definitely corked.

The 1982 Championship made up for that. This was a year when the competition was graced by four great matches any one of which would have been an outstanding final and Lyle played in all of them. His first match was against Faldo who played the last seven holes of the morning round in five under and was six up. The afternoon was surely a formality, except that Lyle is never more dangerous than when he decides to abandon caution and make full use of his enormous talent.

He changed putters at lunch time, parred and halved the first afternoon hole. Then, in the next sixteen holes he had eight birdies. He won 2 and 1. Given the history of antipathy between the two, Faldo simply had nowhere to look. This was capitulation on a grand scale. Only Gary Player in 1965 had ever been more down and still won but his seven down position to Tony Lema with seventeen to play took him to the 37th to repair.

Most golfers would have reacted to such an effort but Lyle, playing the somewhat graceless Raymond Floyd in the next round, was seven under when he shook hands. All Floyd could do was moan that the crowds had twice stopped Lyle's ball from going out of bounds, a totally unfounded complaint.

That win gave Lyle a game against one of golf's gentleman, Tom Kite, who had inflicted a fearsome beating on Lyle in the 1981 Ryder Cup at Walton Heath. On that occasion, when Lyle was eight-under-par the match ended on the sixteenth green. Kite was ten under! So there were points to be made and Lyle made them. He won by 8 and 7 and had the particular pleasure of watching his previous tormentor try to play the then notorious third green. In trying to get a chip up the severe tier in the green, Kite watched the ball come back to his feet three times and wound up with an 8. It put him five down and completely stifled his spirit.

Lyle, though, seemed to draw further strength from these enormous efforts and now faced Ballesteros in the final. Seve had played young American Bobby Clampett on his way there, an American who believed that the game was essentially a logical matter of levers, pulleys and angles. 'I'm looking forward,' said Clampett, 'to seeing why Seve

Isao Aoki, the only Japanese golfer to win the World Match-play. He beat Simon Owen (New Zealand) 3 and 2 in 1978 and lost in the final to Bill Rogers (USA) the following year

A View of Wentworth

THE BURMA ROAD – ONE OF SEVE'S FAVOURITES

Once in a while a golfer discovers a club and a course with which he enjoys an instant affinity. It may be the general ambience, a convivial clubhouse with a wide range of facilities, or simply the sheer quality of the golfing terrain that inspires him to peak performance and sometimes greatness.

Whatever the formula, such enduring harmony between a player and his surroundings is rare. Wentworth is one of the few with a capacity to extract continually the best from the best.

Seve Ballesteros first recognized this phenomenon when he made an all too brief first visit, losing in the opening round of the 1976 World Match-play Championship. His teenage affection, however, has turned over the years to captivation and ultimately to ardent admiration. Seven victories over the West course were of major significance in making Britain's favourite Spaniard the undisputed 'Player of the 1980s'.

Seve's Wentworth roll of honour began in 1980 when he captured the Martini tournament with a panache that added several more platoons to his regiment of fans. The first of five World Match-play titles came twelve months later after a titanic struggle

with Ben Crenshaw following victories over Hale Irwin, Greg Norman and Bernhard Langer. He was 27-under-par for his 130 holes.

Ballesteros has been ever present at the autumn showpiece and rarely misses the opportunity to return for its Spring counterpart, the Volvo PGA Championship, which he claimed in 1991 to the delight of his devoted English 'army'.

'I rate Wentworth at the very top of my list of favourite places alongside Augusta,' says Seve, 'and not just because I play so well there. The Club is warm and friendly and has always treated me well. Of course, I might add the West course is a complete test which requires all the clubs in the bag. The short holes are strong, the long holes reward the genuine long hitter, and the doglegs go both ways. You have to play shots from all kinds of lies, uphill, sidehill and downhill, and also know how to judge the wind swirling in the trees. For me, it is the ultimate examination.'

Ballesteros has hit many memorable strokes at Wentworth. The ones he cherishes are not the obvious examples like the eagle chip-in at the eighteenth against Arnold Palmer in the World Match-play or the extra time 5-iron to master Colin Montgomerie in the 1991 Volvo PGA Championship.

'I remember especially the two 7-iron shots that finished 4 feet from the flags for birdies at the tenth and sixteenth on the afternoon of the 1981 Match-play final against Crenshaw,' he says. 'The first one put me ahead for the first time in the match and having fallen back again the second enabled me to draw level and go on to win. My best putt was the one that beat Sandy Lyle at the 37th the following year – it was all of 40 feet over a sodden green – and my best golf was when I beat Nick Price for my record fifth match-play win. I did not have one bogey in the 34 holes of the final.'

Seve is immensely grateful having the Wentworth stage to show off his golfing talents. 'It is one of the reasons for my success in golf in Britain,' he says. 'The people support me a lot even when I am against British players and I feel at ease and at home. Because of that, I have had the confidence to win three Opens in Britain.'

The Club has reciprocated by making 'Our Seve' an honorary member. Augusta knows it no longer has a monopoly of mutual admiration.

MICHAEL BRITTEN

is such a good player.' Ballesteros won with seven under for the last seventeen holes but if Clampett found out why Seve was such a good player he has never succeeded in putting his discovery to good use.

Lyle fought the most furious of good fights in the final. He had five birdies in the last seven holes of regular play to level matters. Then they went to the 37th. It was bucketing down, squeegees had to be used to clear putting paths and Ballesteros outrageously splashed in a putt from 40 feet at the first extra hole for a winning birdie. It was a spectacular, if monstrously unfair, finish to one of the great Match-play weeks.

Norman won again in 1983, beating Faldo in a final many felt the latter was fortunate to reach. That was the year when Faldo's ball was thrown or kicked back on to the sixteenth green by a partisan spectator so that he won a hole against Graham Marsh which he had looked likely to lose. However, he lost a great deal of sympathy when he refused to say he regretted the manner of his victory, even after

Seve Ballesteros versus Bernhard Langer, 1984

When Seve Ballesteros entered the locker room, his eyes were focused as usual on what lay ahead. By now, Wentworth had practically become the Spaniard's spiritual home. He simply adored the course and it rewarded his devotion with success almost every time he played.

For once, however, the great man's gaze was distracted by a copy of a Sunday newspaper being read by a caddie and in particular by a story previewing that day's final match against Bernhard Langer.

The previous day, the German had talked about his forthcoming match against Seve with unusual, indeed biting, candour. According to Langer, Seve tried to intimidate opponents, was not happy unless other golfers thought he was super and disliked Bernhard because he had voted against Ballesteros's selection for the 1981 Ryder Cup team.

This was serious stuff and Seve's eyes narrowed as he read the article. By the time he arrived on the first tee, Ballesteros was in a thunderous mood. Langer, not an easy man to intimidate, was as curt as his partner. Clearly, this was golf clubs at dawn.

In an atmosphere as cold as a planning meeting at the North Pole, the two men set about their business.

Not a word was exchanged. There was just the blur of steel, the whoosh of a ball taking off, the clicking of a spiked heel on a gravel path. It was drama of the most compelling kind. For once, the cliche about letting your clubs do the talking was appropriate. Langer and Ballesteros each tried to make statements that day. In the end, only Seve succeeded.

His 2 and 1 victory was as much a tribute to his determination as to his play. Every time Langer hit a good shot, Seve seemed to conjure up a great one. And always that dark scowl danced across the Spaniard's face, his bleak mood deepening as the match approached its climax. Although Langer suggested resistance when he eagled the twelfth in the afternoon to move to within one hole of his glowering rival, the result was never seriously in doubt for veteran Seve watchers.

Later in his press interview, Seve claimed teasingly that he had not seen the story and waited for Langer to come and join him before discussing it. The German seemed startled when he came in and saw Seve waiting for him but he defused the situation swiftly enough.

'Maybe I used the wrong word when I said intimidate. Perhaps competitive is a better way to describe Seve,' he admitted. As Langer talked Ballesteros looked, well, to be honest, intimidatingly smug!'

BILL ELLIOTT

115

seeing what happened on television. 'This was the World Match-play,' he said, 'not the Wentworth Christmas Alliance.'

Ballesteros, one down on the last, chipped in against Arnold Palmer for an eagle to take the match on and, with the unkindness of youth, won at the third extra hole. 'I'd like to play him again this afternoon,' said the great but ageing warrior. However, Palmer had played his last World Match-play match.

Norman, never down, cruised to the final, then cruised through it. Only one up after 26 holes, Norman hit a 3-wood second 231 yards to 2 feet, holed for a birdie and went on to win by 4 and 2.

Ballesteros was to win in 1984 which meant that in the 21 years of the event's existence no Briton had taken the title. Gary Player was invited back for the celebratory occasion and in the first round played the Burma Road as if strolling down Memory Lane. He was round in 64 in the morning and the unfortunate Tsuneyuki 'Tommy' Nakajima, six-under-par after 32 holes, lost by 5 and 4.

Player could not keep it up, though, and lost to Norman in the next round. Langer beat Norman but Ballesteros beat Langer to win for the third time in a neither great nor glorious but grim final. He beat him again in 1985 in one of the worst finals of all. If Langer had parred the last five holes he would have had rounds of 76 and 77. That year's event was notable for the match between Ian Woosnam and American Joey Sindelar. The Welshman had eleven birdies and an eagle against the American and still only won by 4 and 2.

By winning the 1985 final Ballesteros had now won fifteen out of his last sixteen matches since 1981. The one he lost was the 1983 semi-final against Norman. Surprisingly, another Australian, Rodger Davis, stopped the sequence. Ballesteros, sallow and off colour, lost 7 and 6 to an opponent who was nine under when he won.

Once again, though, it was Lyle who gave the tournament its impetus. He and Tommy Nakajima featured in a match that was simply breathtaking and the Japanese needed all his inscrutability to take this defeat, especially in view of the manner of it. Nakajima went round the course in 65 and 64 – fifteen-under-par – and lost. Lyle finished birdie, eagle to square the match and then won at the first extra hole, the seventeenth when Nakajima took 6.

It was, however, also too much for Lyle who seemed to have nothing left for the final against Norman. Sandy went to the turn in the morning round in 39 and was, as he ought to have been, five down. He had a short putt to be only two down at the eighteenth but missed. Then Norman rubbed it in by holing from a bunker at the nineteenth to go four up.

The win at least enabled Norman to satisfy his four-year-old daughter, Morgan-Leigh, whose birthday was on the day of the final. When asked what she wanted for a present, she answered, 'the Suntory trophy'.

If only it was always that easy to please little girls.

A View of Wentworth

FOR NORMAN THE WEST IS ALWAYS FUN

Greg Norman is another for whom Wentworth has become synonymous with personal glory. The flaxen-haired Australian rivals Ballesteros and Gary Player for pride of place in the Club's hall of fame after winning the World Match-play title three times in the 1980s and helping as a Volvo Tour member to establish a decade of European mastery over the Americans in the event.

Yet it was his first victory on the West course in 1979 that established Norman's reputation for aggressive golf and led to the subsequent soubriquet of Great White Shark.

The Queenslander had won the Martini tournament on his British debut at Rosemount Blairgowrie in the rain two years earlier. He lost it the following year to Seve Ballesteros but reclaimed the title at Wentworth with a stroke of stupendous power and accuracy that remains a vivid memory both for the fortunate onlookers and Norman a dozen years later.

'It was one of the greatest shots I have hit in my life,' recalls Norman. 'It was at the eighteenth on the last day. Bernhard Langer had finished a shot ahead of me and I needed an eagle 3 to win. I can still remember the yardage like yesterday. I had 243 yards to the flag and I hit a 1-iron about six feet from the hole. I made the putt to win by a shot!'

That smash-and-grab act endeared Norman to the Wentworth galleries who saw him win a third Martini title on the West course in 1981, just a few months after he recorded his inaugural World Match-play victory by beating the Wentworth 'triumvirate' of Nick Faldo, Bernard Gallacher and Sandy Lyle.

Faldo and Ballesteros were among Norman's 1983 match-play victims. Then Jack Nicklaus and Lyle were forced to bend the knee when Norman completed the treble in 1986.

'That is why I always enjoy returning to Wentworth,' he says. 'I have so many fond memories. Whenever you play a course well and have all those good memories your game, even when you are not playing well, gets lifted up. I like the West course and when I am on form I can have a lot of fun making birdies out there.'

What the Australian appreciates especially about the work of architect Harry Colt is the 'flow' of the woodland design. 'He did not move a lot of dirt but just left the mounds there,' he says. 'You go up and over, round and underneath, and it has resulted in a natural progression and a good mixture of short and long holes. I have always found it a very good test of most clubs in the bag with the chance to have fun on the par 5s which all come within the range of two big shots.'

Fun is not the first word the average golfer would choose to describe the severest holes of the famous Burma Road but, then, the aristocrats of the game sometimes have a quirky sense of humour.

MICHAEL BRITTEN

World Match-play
The British take over

MITCHELL PLATTS

It was Ian Woosnam who finally made the break-through for Britain

Severiano Ballesteros is a golfer for all seasons. In winter, he will wander down to the beach near his home in Pedrena, tip a bucket of balls on the golden sands and practise where, as a stripling, he dreamed of the power and glory that was around the corner. In spring, Ballesteros blooms amongst the azaleas and the dogwood at Augusta National where in 1980 and 1983 he won the Masters. In summer, he warms to the task of challenging for the Open Championship wherever that is being played. In autumn, he turns his attention to one course – Wentworth – and the winning of the World Match-play Championship.

Ballesteros made his first appearance in the Championship in 1976. His victories in 1981, 1982, 1984 and 1985 fortified his reputation as the number one golfer. What is more, the wins took the irrepressible Spaniard to the threshold of a dream. He has been galvanized throughout his fabulous career by the desire to establish new records. With four wins in five years, Ballesteros found himself in sight of his target – Gary Player's extraordinary total of five World Match-play Championship triumphs.

Many observers believed Player's total would stand the test of time. Ballesteros felt confident he would equal the record in 1986. He did not. Greg Norman proved as invincible that year as he had in 1980 and 1983. In 1987 these two golfing titans, who together had dominated the Championship for seven years, appeared on course to settle another score intensified by fate and misfortune. Yet the decider, the classic confrontation everyone hoped for, never happened!

Norman had erupted in 1986 with ten victories against Ballesteros's six. It catapulted the Australian to the top of the World rankings leaving Ballesteros kicking his spikes in frustration. That winter he dreamed of taking on Norman at Augusta and when both players found themselves in a play-off it appeared that the script was going according to plan. The record books show that Larry Mize spoiled the scenario. What is more, Ballesteros and Norman were shut out that summer in the other three major championships. So they waited impatiently for autumn and Wentworth and the World Match-play Championship.

On the eve of the 1987 Championship, Ballesteros said, 'There are not many who can win on this golf course. I think Greg and I dominate because of our length. It is a long course, and one which demands that you manufacture a variety of shots.' Norman explained, 'I don't think it's a question of our intimidating others, but more a fact that the course suits our style of play.'

The stage was set, the pair seeded to meet in the final. Yet what unfolded in 1987 served only to strengthen the suggestion, amplified by the success that summer of Nick Faldo in the Open two years after Sandy Lyle had won the title, that the door had swung open on a brave, bright, new era in British golf.

Ian Woosnam exemplified the new spirit, too, and Wentworth provided the stage to prove the point. Norman did not win, neither did Seve. Woosnam took the 24th Championship, beating Lyle in the final to become the first British golfer to pick up the World Match-play Championship trophy. Predictably, his success motivated other British golfers to perform heroic deeds on the West course at Wentworth, but that is getting ahead of ourselves.

Peter German, the International Management Group's Tournament Director, has responsibility each year for running the World Match-play Championship

The greatest storm in 300 years caused devestation but the show went on at Wentworth!

The watershed events of 1987 demand close inspection.

This was the week of 'The Great Storm.' It hit on Thursday night only hours after officials had been compelled to suspend play in the first round because of prolonged downpours. The forecasters gave no warning of what was to come and admitted it was the worst storm for three hundred years. Lives were lost, hundreds of thousands of trees uprooted, cars were smashed, people were told to stay indoors for their own safety and even then some houses were wrecked by falling trees. When dawn broke the storm was still raging.

Ballesteros, however, zigzagged his way to the Club between the fallen trees, the legacy of the overnight havoc, as did the other players. No one failed to make it on a day when South East England ground to a halt! Graphically, Ballesteros likened it to being 'in Vietnam without guns.' However, he was as ill-prepared for a round of golf as he had ever been. Ballesteros had not slept because of the howling wind, and had walked to the course with his brother Vicente. 'We were very careful and worried because of the possibility of more trees coming down on top of us,' he recalled.

That the first round was completed on Friday was, indeed, a miracle. The green staff and the organizers were rightly applauded for their marvellous efforts.

That year, Norman was not involved in first round action in which Seve had beaten the Japanese golfer Katsunari Takahashi in a match that lasted two days because of the storm. Norman only joined

Ian Woosnam versus Sandy Lyle, 1987

Wentworth resembled a battlefield in the autumn of 1987. The hurricane that had devastated much of southern England had not ignored the Virginia Water estate, its glorious gardens, its even more glorious golf courses. Just gaining entrance to the Club was a major task with trees lying like so many pathetic, stricken giants, cut down in their prime by a wind that howled like a banshee before ripping into the woods. It meant that play on the second day was impossible. Instead, the fairways echoed plaintively to the sound of chain saws rather than the applause of an appreciative gallery.

It was, however, an exciting as well as a heartbreaking time. No one caught in this awesome wind will ever forget its raw power but by Monday's delayed final the golf offered a rival for the memory banks. Woosnam versus Lyle was, to put it mildly, one heck of a match! In prospect and in fact.

Lyle was already an Open champion. Meanwhile, Woosnam had taken four European Tour titles on his way to the West course that season. Sandy had proved himself to be genuine world class and Woosnam was on the very edge of achieving the same accolade.

One other thing; their presence in the final meant that Britain was at last guaranteed a winner in the World Match-play! We had waited 24 years to hail one of our own and now the moment had arrived. Popular sentiment rested with Lyle who was appearing remarkably in his fourth final but Woosnam was in startling and resolute form when this inevitably calm October Monday dawned. They had played together or against each other as amateurs – now they were opponents in one of the world's greatest golf tournaments.

The match turned out to be as good natured as it

in at round two as one of the four seeds and suffered the same fate as the other three – Open champion Nick Faldo, Masters champion Larry Mize and US Open champion Scott Simpson. Unprecedentedly, the top four seeds all lost – Norman to the Zimbabwean Mark McNulty on the last green. For the first time, too, the four semi-finalists – Seve, Ian Woosnam, Sandy Lyle and McNulty, were all regulars from Europe's Volvo Tour.

'I've been saying for some time now that the Europeans have been getting better and better. People used to laugh at me but it is nice to be proved right,' said Ballesteros, hopeful that he would land that record equalling fifth title at the expense of Woosnam in the semi-final, then either Lyle or McNulty in the final.

Norman had threatened never to come back because of what he considered biased crowds. Now, he slipped away quietly, chuntering that it was wrong that some played four ties and others only three because of the twelve man format. He would prefer it to be eight as it used to be. As far as Seve was concerned, his great rival was now out of the way. But it was not to be Seve year's either.

Seve went out in the semi-final to Woosnam who had matched the Spaniard's 70 in the morning and shot 67 to win one up in the afternoon. The game was not without incident. Woosnam had moved three up by the seventh in the afternoon but after 35 holes the match was square again. Both Woosnam and Seve drove into the trees but the Welshman's ball hit a branch and dropped on a muddy path from

was impressive. Though the stakes were scarily high, the opportunity to make a real mark in the history of British golf was a compelling one. There was, however, nothing but sportsmanship and professional competitiveness.

Each hailed the other's good shots. And there was plenty to hail with both men still locked in overdrive despite the rigours they had undergone in actually making it to the final. Woosnam, three up with two to play in the morning round, seemed set to lunch on a significant lead but Lyle, entirely typically, birdied the seventeenth hole and then almost casually eagled the eighteenth to bite on his sandwich just one down on the 'wee fella'. Each had gone round in a four-under-par 68 – as close as scoring can be marked in match-play where putts are given.

The afternoon dogfight was even closer. Woosnam edged ahead, Lyle clawed back. By the time they stood on the seventeenth tee again they were all square. Nothing changed and each had a birdie 4 at

this beautiful beast of a dogleg.

Now only the eighteenth remained if the match was to finish in normal time. Significantly, the chatting had long since ceased.

Lyle, by dint of a birdie at the sixteenth, drove first and drove well. Woosnam followed suit. As a pale sun squinted through the sky, the Welshman then hit his shot of the week, a rifled 3-wood that struck the heart of the green.

Lyle's response was a 2-iron approach that wobbled with uncertainty before plunging into a bunker from where he took three to get down. Woosnam comfortably made his two putt birdie and began celebrating with his familiar punch into the cool air. It was a fitting end to a match that lived up to public expectation. Britain – and Wales especially – had its champion at last.

BILL ELLIOTT

*Nick Faldo has won the World
Match-play Championship twice*

which he gained relief. He hit a 1-iron short of the green. Ballesteros
had hit the fairway with a towering drive and, mindful of the fact that
he had hit two drivers in the morning and made a birdie, he pulled out
his driver again. It was a gamble which did not pay off.

The ball flew deep into the trees and, although he got relief from
storm damage, he did not like the lie at the point where he had
dropped the ball. It was on a path strewn with straw. Andy McFee, the
referee, was adamant he play from that spot but Seve asked for a
second opinion and received a further drop from chief referee Tony
Gray. The Spaniard chipped to 6 feet but missed. Woosnam, 5 feet
away, holed and the hopes of a dream final between Norman and
Ballesteros had been well and truly shattered. Now both were out!

By the time the final came along on the Monday Woosnam,
following victories over Faldo and Ballesteros, was ready to rule the

Sandy Lyle was in four finals before he won the title in 1988

World or, at the very least, the World Match-play Championship. The Welshman did too, although it was a close affair. Lyle, who had taken care of McNulty in the semi-finals, won three of the last four holes in the morning to lunch one up. Woosnam, two down with eleven to play, decided to stand taller over his putts. The manoeuvre transformed his touch. He holed from 12 feet at the eighth – the 26th – and from 40 feet two holes later. They came to the last all square and Woosnam made British golfing history by holing from 6 feet to win with a birdie.

Lyle's turn arrived twelve months later. The silver anniversary edition of the Championship produced another all British final and Lyle, with a performance that sparkled like the golden hues of autumn, beat Faldo 2 and 1. Lyle had won the Masters that year and he was on a high. He thrashed Ballesteros 7 and 6 in the semi-finals to end the Spaniard's hopes that year of a fifth title win. Faldo, however, was also playing well as his earlier last hole win against Woosnam, the defending champion, had illustrated. Lyle was eager to erase the bitter experience of having lost on each of the previous four occasions that he had featured in the final and it showed. He gathered twelve birdies and one eagle in a final which once again was held over to the Monday because of a deluge the previous day.

In the morning, Lyle gained a two hole advantage mostly because of his authority on the greens. He single-putted eleven times. Faldo missed six times from inside 10 feet. Lyle even had the gall to leave his putter in the bag at the eighteenth, where he chipped in from 20 yards to halve the hole.

Even so, Faldo was square after three holes in the afternoon. A fascinating confrontation was turning into a titanic final of rare drama and style. Faldo led for the first time at the tenth – the 28th – and looked like going further ahead four holes later when he hit a 5-iron to 10 feet at the short fourteenth with Lyle 32 feet away. Lyle, however, won the hole, coaxing his putt home while Faldo missed.

Lyle edged one up again at the fifteenth. Faldo holed from 7 feet for a birdie at the next. Lyle followed him in. True to character, Lyle made life difficult for himself at the seventeenth. He reached the green with a drive and a glorious 2-iron – but he hit his first putt 14 feet past. Lyle had to hole to end the match and, of course, he did.

However, Faldo's turn came in 1989 and, as with Woosnam and Lyle, success in the World Match-play Championship provided the finishing stroke to a year of great achievement. That year Faldo won the Masters and in Europe he captured the Volvo PGA Championship at Wentworth, the Dunhill British Masters and the Peugeot French Open. Finally, he returned to the West course to overcome Woosnam following a wonderful week in which he was 38-under-par. Indeed, Faldo was compelled to play the final nine holes in 30, a record for the event, recovering from three down with seven to play.

The way in which Faldo had fought back was reminiscent of the magnificent manner in which he had dramatically clawed his way back to win the Masters earlier in the year. He demonstrated again what a master of escapology he is, leaving Woosnam deflated, disappointed and beaten!

A year later, Woosnam was all smiles when he became the first British player to win the World Match-play Championship twice! The little Welshman began the week by revealing that he had pulled a muscle in his groin and that unless it improved he would be unable to walk 36 holes each day. However, heat treatment worked wonders for Woosie and he was required to walk only 34 holes in the final as he beat Mark McNulty 4 and 2.

The British stranglehold on the World Match-play Champion-ship had served to thwart Ballesteros's bid for a record equalling fifth triumph but in 1991 the Spaniard made no mistake. He reached the final and beat Nick Price 3 and 2 with golf of the highest calibre. He shot 65 in the morning, lunching all square, and played the next sixteen holes in 59 strokes to end Price's brave resistance. Furthermore, Ballesteros completed the final without dropping a shot to equal a record set in 1971 by the only other five times winner, Gary Player. Ballesteros, of course, was delighted. 'I know this course as well as my course at home in Pedrena,' he said. 'I love this Championship.'

However, his win failed to satisfy his hunger. He arrived back at Wentworth in 1992 and despite an indifferent year was convinced that the intoxicating atmosphere of the World Match-play Championship would drive him towards that record sixth win. It was not to be. Jeff Sluman of the United States bundled Ballesteros out of the Championship in the second round and Faldo won the title for a second time when he beat Sluman 8 and 7 in a one-sided final.

Ballesteros returned home. It was wintertime again. Time to make for the golden sands and hone his game for another year, time to relive the memories, the good and the bad. Time to look forward, too, to the Masters, to the Open and, of course, to golf's autumn extravaganza – the World Match-play Championship on the West course at Wentworth and to dream of a record sixth victory.

Nick Faldo versus Ian Woosnam, 1989

Timing his move to perfection, Nick Faldo won the Championship for the first time when he defeated Ian Woosnam in a final of the highest quality.

Faldo was behind until the 36th hole where he produced an eagle 3 to trump Woosnam's birdie. The Ryder Cup partners burned up the Burma Road but at the end it was Faldo who had the overdrive. He came home in a record 30 strokes for a round of 64.

For the 105 holes he played in the Championship he was 38-under-par, matchless scoring in the 25 year history of the competition. Faldo, who had begun the year by winning the US Masters, won £100,000 at Wentworth and donated it all to children's charities.

Woosnam, the champion in 1987, had gone out in the morning in 32 and had been three up after eagling the twelfth. Faldo had begun to judge every shot on a scale of 1 to 10, however, and was now aiming to hit golf's equivalent of Bo Derek on every hole! 'All I see is the pin, no trees, no bunkers,' he said.

At lunch, Woosnam was one up after Faldo had birdies at the fifteenth and sixteenth and an eagle at the seventeenth but the Englishman was to produce an even deadlier finish in the afternoon.

Woosnam re-established a three hole lead but Faldo struck at the twelfth, the 30th of the match, with a putt of 38 feet for an eagle. At the next he hit a 9-iron to 4 feet. A platinum blonde who had her view obscured by a cameraman yelled 'on yer bike' to the photographer and Faldo laughed for the first time.

He was now only one down and he levelled at the 34th. Woosnam had Faldo at his mercy at the 35th, hitting a 3-iron with laser beam accuracy from 240 yards to 10 feet. Faldo missed the green to the right but he got up and down for 4 while Woosnam missed his putt for an eagle 3.

There was nothing wrong with the way the Welshman played the last but Faldo played it better. He hit a magnificent 1-iron to the heart of the green and sank the 20-foot eagle putt. For the first and only time Faldo was up, and there were no more holes to play!

TIM GLOVER

A View of Wentworth

LYLE HAS A SCORE TO SETTLE

Sandy Lyle, like Nick Faldo, Gary Player, Seve Ballesteros, Ian Woosnam and Greg Norman, is proud to be an honorary member of Wentworth Club.

The 1985 Open champion, Lyle lived on the course before he decided to move with his wife Jolande and family north to Scotland. He is another longtime admirer of Colt's masterpiece, the West course but at one stage in his career he must have felt that he was never going to win over it.

Four times between 1980 and 1987 he battled his way through to the final of the World Match-play only to lose – twice to Greg Norman and once each to Seve Ballesteros and Ian Woosnam. It seemed as if he was jinxed at Wentworth until in 1988 he had the satisfaction of beating Nick Faldo 2 and 1 in the final.

'The course is always challenging,' says Lyle. 'I'll admit I was more used to playing much more open courses than the Burma Road and frankly it was quite a strain for me – still is – to keep out of the trees!

'What playing at Wentworth has done, however, is sharpen up my ability to hit straighter shots off the tee! Assuming I hit straight, and because I'm a longer hitter than many, the West suits my game. On the other hand, I may just think that because in Match-play you can get away with five bogeys as long as you have ten birdies!

'There are some magnificent holes on the course, not least the opening hole and the eighteenth. That opening tee shot is not as frightening as some others because it is to a more open fairway but it is the second shot, often into the wind, that is a real tester, more so because it comes so early in the round. Playing a medium to long iron over the valley to a putting surface bunkered left and right quickly concentrates the mind. You don't ease into Wentworth; the challenge is there from the start. Indeed, there are not too many holes where you can relax.

'Arguably, the eighteenth is a comfortable par 5 but under pressure at the end of a round and needing a birdie to win or force a play-off it is a cracker. Hit your drive into the trees on the right and you are dead; hit the fairway right close to the woods and you can be so effectively blocked out that you have little or no chance of reaching the green in two; finish in the left rough and you can lose control of the second shot as you go for the green over the bunker on the left that guards the putting surface! There have been some magnificent eagles at the hole but some high numbers too. It's a suitably demanding finishing hole to what I have always considered a supreme golfing examination.

'What I enjoy about playing at Wentworth, too, is the atmosphere. Because of the trees, the crowds are reasonably close to the action and their cheers are accentuated by the trees. The events staged at Wentworth – the World Match-play and the Volvo PGA – are among the most prestigious outside the Open, so the crowds are always large and enthusiastic. From a player's point of view, I feel Wentworth always gives you a very special feeling. So much tradition and history have been packed into the comparatively short, 70-year history of the Club that I sometimes think of it in the same affectionate way that I think of the Old course at St Andrews.

'In the old days the course could become very hard and bouncy during a dry spell – conditions that made it easier for me to end up in the trees – but now that they have one of the most sophisticated watering systems, the West is always in good condition.

'Softer fairways and rough stop the balls running into the trees which in places are so condensed that you have difficulty swinging the club as you line up your recovery shot. People sometimes forget about the drainage ditches in there, too. Sometimes they are hidden. The course has magnificently stood the test of time and does not need to be tampered with in any way but if there was a minor improvement that ought to be made I feel it should be to expose those ditches more by cutting back the branches of the trees on the edge of the rough to a height of six or seven feet. They regularly do this kind of thing in America.

'You know, one of the most important factors at Wentworth, and one reason why it takes some getting used to, is the wind. It can completely disorient you. You can glance up at the clouds and see them scudding along in one direction while at ground level the wind is blowing the other way. The confusion makes club selection tough at times and those who know the course well and have played it many times have a distinct advantage over first-timers.'

In the days when he was an estate resident, Sandy, always relaxed and easy-going, had the luxury of being able to stroll across the East course to keep his West course tee off time. His caddie would drive round with the bag and be waiting for him on the tee. He has always enjoyed playing the course although he has one disappointment about his form at Wentworth.

'I love the place but I have never done well there in stroke-play tournaments. I've had far too many early tee off times on the third and fourth days I'm afraid. I've had my chances, of course, like in 1985 when I lost the PGA Championship title to Paul Way at the third extra hole.

'I was two ahead with three to play but we both finished on 282. I had a chance to finish him off at the second hole of the play-off but missed a four-footer and he beat me at the next – the long dogleg left seventeenth. I remember he did not hit his drive all that well but got away with it because the ball went right rather than left. He then hit a magnificent, championship winning 3-wood to the back apron and made a birdie.

'As for shots I've been proud of hitting at Wentworth, I remember a 4-iron I hit in one of my matches with Nick Faldo in the World Match-play. I was one up playing the fifteenth hole and was faced with the demanding prospect of having to hit a 190 yards second shot. It was a crucial stage in the match and I can recall it vividly. The ball finished 4 feet from the pin!

'That shot gave me tremendous satisfaction but I'll not be really happy until I have won a stroke-play title round the West.

'Then Wentworth and I will really be at peace with each other!'

RENTON LAIDLAW

Sandy Lyle delighted at one of his 1983 victories in the World Match-play – but he did not win the final

European Tour

RENTON LAIDLAW

Four men were involved in the inspired move that brought the PGA European Tour to Wentworth in 1981 – Neil Coles, Chairman of the Tour, Bernard Gallacher, the Wentworth Club Professional, Ken Schofield, the Tour's Executive Director and, perhaps most significantly, Richard Doyle-Davidson, then Secretary of the Wentworth Club. Doyle-Davidson had arrived at Wentworth in 1977 from Formby on the Lancashire coast, eager to get down to the task of restoring some of the Club's lost prestige by building on the solid foundation laid by the annual staging of the World Match-play Championship since 1964.

It was clear the Tour was outgrowing its London headquarters. Space at the Tour's Oval Cricket Ground offices was tight even after the split from the PGA in 1976 when the Club Professionals had moved off to a new home at The Belfry. The Tournament Players

Division had remained in London, operating outside the PGA umbrella as a fully autonomous organization – an inevitable move at a time when the game was enjoying an unprecedented boom.

Today, the two branches of professional golf combine successfully to run the Ryder Cup sponsored by Johnnie Walker. They develop independently, but in complementary fashion, all facets of professional golf with Scot Sandy Jones in charge of the club side of the business and Schofield masterminding the tournament players scene.

Back in 1976, however, as Seve Ballesteros was winning the first of his to date 52 PGA European and Volvo Tour titles, and Nick Faldo, Sandy Lyle, Bernhard Langer and Ian Woosnam were waiting in the wings to burst on the scene, the Tour was thinking how best to expand and in which direction. Informally, Gallacher, Schofield and Coles may well have thought about Wentworth as a potential site for new headquarters. Coles had always enjoyed playing Wentworth and Gallacher, after all, was the highly respected Club Professional. Maybe Gallacher casually planted the seed in Doyle-Davidson's mind. Maybe it was already there because there had been newspaper reports about how fast the Tour, far smaller then than it is now, was outgrowing its headquarters at the Oval. At the time, there was a big drive to weld together a tournament programme that encompassed not just Britain and Ireland but the whole of Europe as well. Larger accommodation was needed to house the extra staff required to make a fully integrated European Tour work.

This was a far from easy task because of the character and independent nature of the various ruling bodies in Europe with whom negotiations had to take place. It had been started by the

Neil Coles, MBE,
Chairman, PGA European Tour
Board of Directors

A View of Wentworth

WOOSNAM AND FALDO AGREE WEST IS BEST

Ian Woosnam and Nick Faldo stand at opposite ends of the professional line — and for far more reasons than that one is 5ft 4in. tall and the other 6ft 3in. They have different life styles, attitudes and swings but there is a common bond and a strong one at that. They share a deep-rooted affection for Wentworth's Burma Road. And for both, it was love at first sight.

Woosnam was hardly known outside his own farmyard, never mind Shropshire, when he first made his way through the beautiful and luxurious estate and teed off into golfing ecstasy. He had heard much about the course but had never seen it. So while playing at nearby Foxhills in the late 1970s he decided to make the short journey over just to see why so many consider the West course one of the best in the world.

In typical streaky Woosnam fashion — for when his putter is hot the gallery needs fire protection outfits — the would-be likely lad birdied four of the first five holes. 'I said to myself immediately this is my kind of course,' recalls the amiable Welshman.

Faldo agrees that the beauty of Wentworth is instantly apparent. 'There is a natural flow and it has a fantastic layout. The course meanders along so superbly.'

The course repaid neither Faldo nor Woosnam for their initial adoration, however — both missed the cut in the 1979 Martini International. Indeed, for Woosnam it would be a painful courtship, taking him five years and nine rounds before he broke par for the first time in tournament play.

Woosnam's record since, however, has been almost unbelievable. Of 32 medal rounds only two have been above par. He has won three events including two World Match-plays, finished second twice and been third on another two occasions. But it says much about the course that although Woosnam has carved some amazing statistics on the Burma Road he has never humiliated it — a 66 in the 1991 Volvo PGA Championship standing as his best medal round.

Faldo needed eleven attempts to break par but once he had done so his statistics became staggering. So much so that in every event since 1983 Faldo has only once finished outside the top ten and it is five years since he last failed to beat par. Three wins have come in the last four seasons and his scoring record includes two seven-under-par 65s.

No wonder both Faldo and Woosnam love the place — although the former, ever the perfectionist, briefly had a period when he was less than satisfied with the condition of the course.

Faldo voiced his opinions and they drifted into the right ears. An automated watering system now ensures that the only comments to be heard today are along the lines of 'never seen it look better.'

The best golfers prefer the hardest courses because they feel that when the premium is on playing a variety of shots, as well as demanding expert course management, they have an advantage over the rest. Few play their way around Wentworth better and although Woosnam may always look as if he is in a hurry to get home, he has one of the most acute golfing brains on tour.

'It can inspire me when I know I am about to play Wentworth,' says Woosnam. 'You have to draw the ball on some shots and fade it on others. What makes it such a good course is that you have to use every club in the bag and every shot in the game.'

The course could have no finer testimony.

MARTIN HARDY

visionary John Jacobs and was being carried on very successfully by his successor Schofield. He had once been the youngest Trustee Savings Bank manager in Scotland before moving to London, initially to work for journalist George Simms who ran London's best known golfing public relations operation. Later, having outgrown that role, he joined Jacobs at the Tour following the split from the PGA. He took over from Jacobs as Executive Director in 1975.

During the 1977 Uniroyal tournament at Moor Park in which Ballesteros beat Faldo in a play-off, Schofield travelled to Wentworth for a meeting and bumped into Doyle-Davidson. A friendship was formed and much later Doyle-Davidson raised tentatively but seriously the question of using the Club as a base for the Tour's administration. Permission to construct a custom-built headquarters in the green belt at Wentworth was not likely to be forthcoming from the local planners but Doyle-Davidson saw the potential of converting a building behind the main clubhouse as a headquarters.

'Richard showed considerable imagination,' says Schofield. 'The two-storey building we were talking about was close to derelict on the ground floor. The part used by the Artisans Club (now disbanded) as clubrooms was fine. But at the other end, George Hammond of Carreras kept the necessary paraphernalia – signs, scoreboards, ropes and stakes, etc – that he needed for the autumn staging of the Piccadilly World Match-play Championship. Above were two flats used by the Club's Head Greenkeeper, the late Gerry Coley, and the Assistant Secretary. 'Richard, being a very practical person, asked how much space the Tour would need at Wentworth to replace the small reception area, the three rooms and two open plan areas which had been home for us at the Oval since 1970.'

In those days, the combined field and office staff of the Tour was around a dozen people, a fifth of today's staff operating from Wentworth and initially, Doyle-Davidson and Coles felt that use of part of the lower half of the Wentworth building would be sufficient to fulfil the Tour's requirements. Doyle-Davidson set about making space available by relocating the Artisans and finding somewhere else to store the World Match-play equipment. For its part, the Tour showed its excitement about the possibility of a link with Wentworth by bringing Tour golf back to the course by scheduling the Martini event for a spring date which effectively complemented the Club's autumn World Match-play fixture.

Schofield recalls, 'There was never a question of our going elsewhere. We knew that the timing for the Tour to move was right, that to move to a golfing centre was sensible and that there was no better centre we could go to than highly reputable Wentworth.'

It has always been a happy marriage.

Having decided in principle to accept the offer from Wentworth, the Tour's friends at the Oval were informed. The move would not happen overnight. In fact, the whole business took almost four years to complete. It was evident that the cricketing authorities, with whom the Tour has always had an excellent relationship, were sorry about the news. However, the move made it easier for them to pursue their own expansion plans.

Doyle-Davidson and Coles got down to detailed planning and decided that to use only a part of the ground floor was not practical for an organization that was growing so rapidly. Realistic predictions of the space requirement for the next few years resulted in the revised view that it would be wiser to take over the whole of the bottom floor.

Wentworth was so convinced that having the Tour as tenant would be good for the Club, that it provided the accommodation at a peppercorn rent and spent £10,000 preparing the shell of the building for the Tour to fit out on its arrival. In the Spring of 1981 the Tour moved in. Marina Bray, Ken Schofield's Personal Assistant, and Gillian Oosterhuis, supervised the move over the Easter Weekend.

'Two companies helped us furnish the new headquarters, Shell, with whom we still have a private day with our Board each year, and Hennessy, involved at the time in its own Cup competition with us,' recalls Schofield. 'Together they put up £45,000 to fit, furnish and decorate our new stockbroker belt home, acquired initially on a long lease.'

The Fairclough company owned Wentworth at the time but later amalgamated with William Press to become AMEC plc. Neil Macfarlane, later to spend a spell as Minister for Sport in one of Lady Thatcher's governments, eventually becoming Sir Neil, was on the Wentworth Board in the late 1980s when AMEC decided to offer the Tour the opportunity to buy its offices.

Realizing how good both the Tour and the Club were for each other, Macfarlane, in particular, helped negotiate the sale. However, before the deal was signed AMEC sold out to the property company Chelsfield in a very quickly organized hush-hush deal.

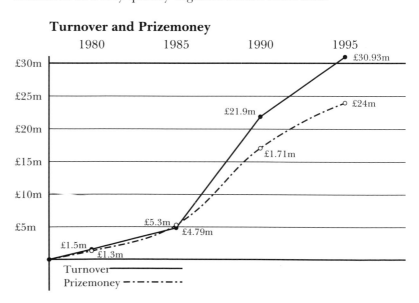

The success graphs of the PGA European Tour

'It might have been awkward but the AMEC board, to their eternal credit, made it quite clear to Chelsfield that since tacit agreement had been reached to sell the property to us, the deal should not be jeopardized. Chelsfield happily agreed,' says Schofield.

Today, the Tour owns the whole building it moved into in 1981 and plans have already been passed to allow for further important, if limited, expansion. In addition, a new branch office has been opened at nearby Chobham.

With easy access to Heathrow, one of the busiest airline hubs of Europe, those doing business for and with the Tour have found getting to and from Wentworth comparatively easy. The airport is less than 30 minutes away from the offices of Schofield, George O'Grady, the Deputy Executive Director and Managing Director of the vital marketing wing of the Tour – PGA European Tour Enterprises – and Richard Hills who is closely involved with the development of another branch of Tour business – properties. This is allied to the golf course designing and building partnership set up in 1992 between the Tour and the International Management Group. Neil Coles and Peter Townsend, a former PGA champion, and Colin Maclaine, a former

Top executives of the PGA European Tour meet at Wentworth.
(from left to right) Ken Schofield (Executive Director), John Paramor, Marina Bray, Richard Hills, George O'Grady (Managing Director Tour Enterprises), Tony Gray, Mitchell Platts and Michael Friend

top amateur player, head this division.

The Tour has another partnership venture, too, with TWI the television film branch of IMG, Mark McCormack's multifaceted organisation. PGA European Tour Productions is geared to expanding and improving television coverage of over 40 events annually and of giving golf fans a deeper insight into the game and of the men who play it for a living.

At Wentworth, Tony Gray runs the expanding Senior Tour which is sure to blossom when Tony Jacklin turns 50 in 1994. Andy Stubbs has responsibility for the 35 tournament strong Challenge Tour which gives vital competitive experience to younger players aspiring to full Tour status, and experienced John Paramor has a twofold role at headquarters – Chief Referee and Field Operations Director in which his right hand men are senior Tournament Directors Michael Stewart and Andy McFee along with David Garland, David Probyn and Stubbs. Another PGA European Tour official, Michael Tate, is in charge of the Ryder Cup, and Bruce Jamieson and Richard Stillwell head the agronomy division that has done so much to improve and upgrade the condition of the courses visited by the Volvo Tour each year.

English may remain the language of golf in Europe but the Tour staff is multilingual. Certain staff members are fluent in French and German, Spanish and Italian, and Continental field staff are now helping to run tournaments, making it easier to talk to players in their own languages and explain rules and decisions made during tournaments.

Wentworth is so convenient for Europe that it has not been necessary for the Tour, which gained a vital corporate sponsor in Volvo in 1988 allowing it to continue its expansion programme, to go to the expense of setting up branch offices in every European capital. For Schofield, who visits between two thirds and three quarters of all Tour events each year, and O'Grady or any of the other senior staff, the quick unscheduled trip to the Continent for a vital meeting is no hassle from Wentworth.

With just one brief gap, Tour golf has been staged every year at Wentworth since the Tour moved in and today the West course is the permanent home of the flagship event – the £700,000 Volvo PGA Championship.

There is little doubt that the Tour's arrival at Wentworth, inspired by the initial enthusiasm of Bernard Gallacher, Neil Coles and Richard Doyle-Davidson, has helped extend the Club's international reputation to the point where it is now better known worldwide than it ever has been in its 70-year history.

The advantage to the Tour from a marketing and public relations standpoint of being based at Wentworth is equally apparent.

'There is no better address in golf than Wentworth, Virginia Water, Surrey,' says Tour boss Schofield. 'It is internationally identifiable with the very best of British and European golf at every level.'

There is no doubt that the partnership between the two organizations, now twelve years old, dedicated to promoting their businesses with maximum efficiency but without sacrificing quality and style, works exceptionally well.

Those involved initially in bringing the two together can feel justifiably proud of their matchmaking achievement.

Zimbabwe's Tony Johnstone en route to his 1992 Volvo PGA victory hits his second to the last

A View of Wentworth

FOR GARY A HOST OF HAPPY MEMORIES

'Wentworth is part of me. So much has happened to me there that it will forever have a place in my heart. What a wonderful place to play golf. Just to be there delights me. I know you could say I am a bit of a freak but, unlike many of my colleagues, I take a particular interest in the trees, the water, the flowers and even the rocks on the golf courses I play around the world, and Wentworth has so much to offer. To be honest, it is a pleasure just walking round there.

Harry Colt designed a gem – a course that tests every club in the bag and forces you to play every type of shot. I won five World Match-play titles there and had some victories I will never forget. Great memories, they say, are the cushions of life and I have many from Wentworth; beating Jack Nicklaus twice, Arnold Palmer and on one occasion the great Australian Peter Thomson by 10 and 8.

The West course is such a marvellous venue for match-play and I am such a fan of man to man competition. I remember so vividly some of the incidents,

some of the shots I have played and one match in particular that everyone else remembers too; the one in which I came back from seven down with seventeen to play to beat the American Tony Lema.

I remember that against Lema I missed lunch to practise to try to cure my hook. My wife brought me a cup of tea and a piece of bread before the afternoon round started and, do you know, I hooked the opening tee shot of the afternoon round into a bush and lost the hole. Gradually, however, I began to chip away at Tony's lead and was only one down coming to the 35th hole of the match. People often forget that I had to hole a seven-footer on that green to stay alive there but they, and I, will never forget the 3-wood second shot I played in dampish weather at the last hole to square the match. It was one of the shots of my golfing career. I bent it round the trees and bounced it up and on to the green, 20 feet from the stick. I won the hole and took the tie at the 37th.

I can honestly say I was drained. I was so close to physical collapse that I cried and fell to the ground through sheer exhaustion. Yet I came back next day as strongly as ever. I have been blessed with tremendous energy all my life, more energy than most athletes. I am very fortunate to have such a strong constitution because I have probably travelled more than any other sportsman. Recently, I worked out that I had clocked up no less than eight million miles and spent three of my 57 years sitting 35,000 feet above the earth in aeroplane seats!

Today, far from easing up, my schedule is more hectic than ever. I still play golf around the world and I am busy building courses throughout Asia where the game is booming – and that includes China. Of course, I am building courses, driving ranges and golf academies in the more established golfing countries, too. I hardly have a day off and I love it.

As far as my golf course design work is concerned, I cannot say that I have ever copied any of the holes on the West course but, consciously and sometimes subconsciously, I have used the ideas behind them and I have followed Colt's philosophy.

You can imagine how delighted I was, therefore, to be invited to act as one of the consultants on the newest of the Wentworth courses, the Edinburgh. John Jacobs was the designer and I put forward some ideas on how I felt the course should be shaped and on how I thought the greens should be built. Some of the ideas were picked up, others were not but it is a fine course which fits in well in a glorious stretch of golfing country. If Chelsfield, with whom I am working elsewhere in the world, ever wants to build a fourth course at Wentworth I would love to be given the chance to do it.

I like the area so much that if I did not live where I do in South Africa I would live at Wentworth. I once very nearly bought a house on the course when the houses there were very much cheaper than they are today! I feel so at home in the area. Of course, I have been playing golf there since I first came to England in 1955 with my father. I lived in 17s 6d bed and breakfast lodgings and used to go to Beatie's restaurant in Sunningdale for tea. It no longer exists. I remember, too, marvellous lunches at Wentworth and one in particular at which I smeared lashings of peanut butter on my bread only to find that it was horseradish sauce.

It was at Wentworth where I was once photographed outside the clubhouse entrance with a beauty queen. The photograph, I recall, went round the world and Vivienne, my girl friend back in South Africa who later became my wife, was most put out!

But mostly, I think about the golf. The sound of the loudspeaker calling us to the tee for a tense match-play tie and the crowds there even if it was foggy or frosty or rainy. I once practised alone in the rain before a World Match-play and, do you know, the gallery was huge and stayed with me for all eighteen holes. It was wonderful. The Wentworth spectators are not fair weather fans.

Talking of practising, I once remember Alf Sutton, the Club's locker room attendant, coming out in the dark to ask how much longer I would be. I was hitting balls towards my caddy, identifiable only by the light of the torch he was holding!

As five times winner of the World Match-play in a nine year spell, I love Wentworth and I am delighted that they have installed a watering system to protect the course against those summer droughts that crop up from time to time. That is money well spent. I am now an honorary member of the Club that has meant so much to me and whose members have always been so kind and considerate. I am not back as often as I once was but Went-worth will live forever in my mind as one of the world's great courses with, for me, a stack of happy memories.'

Gary Player in action in the first World Match-play in 1964 watched by eventual winner Arnold Palmer

A New Owner

JOHN HOPKINS

I t was hot that summer of 1988 and Elliott Bernerd was enjoying himself cruising off the coast of France. Until, that is, he was forced to return to London because the boat broke down. Having to cut short his holiday was the bad news. It was quickly followed by the good news.

Back in London, he wondered how best to use a week in which he had no appointments. Bernerd, the Chairman of Chelsfield, the property group, received a telephone call from a business associate. It was a call that changed his life and took him into a new world – the world of golf. Before he received that call Bernerd had no more than a passing interest in golf. But the moment he put down the phone he was on his way to becoming Chairman and owner of the prestigious, world renowned Wentworth Club set in 800 acres of rolling, wooded Surrey countryside. Down the years its West course has staged 100 major tournaments including the Ryder Cup, Curtis Cup, Canada Cup – the forerunner of the World Cup – and each autumn since the early 1960s, the World Match-play Championship. Elliott Bernerd knew that.

At the time of the telephone call to Bernerd, Chelsfield had no plans to move into golf. The company was very much Elliott Bernerd's, founded by him in 1986, the year he became Chairman of the Trustees of the London Symphony Orchestra.

Bernerd was born in 1945 and trained first in a firm of commercial estate agents before setting up his own business which was later bought by Town City Properties. He quickly acquired a reputation for being one of the greatest deal makers of his day. This was because he put together a group of investors to acquire a near bankrupt company which owned the site of Stockley Business Park near Heathrow Airport which was sold three years later in a deal which is said to have given him a personal profit of £20 million.

His entrepreneurial skills were further emphasized in May 1992 when he received £10 million from a Middle East businessman for the leasehold of his magnificent flat in Eaton Square, a flat he had bought and converted for £3 million five years earlier.

At the time he received the tip-off about Wentworth, Bernerd knew little more about Wentworth than that it was a golf club. He was a skier and a tennis player, not a golfer. Nevertheless, the idea of owning such a well known and well located club as Wentworth fascinated him. Was Chelsfield interested in buying? Indeed it was!

'A number of aspects immediately appealed to me,' said Bernerd. 'I liked its location inside the golden triangle between the M4 and the M3. I liked its reputation and what Wentworth stood for – the brand name and its standing in the golf world, internationally and domestically. The name is recognizable in almost every country in Europe, the Far East and in America. It had a limited number of corporate memberships and we felt that the whole corporate area could be improved upon. I felt it had enormous potential.

'Moreover, it was a proprietor's not a member's club. This allowed us to act in a proprietorial fashion. And I thought that because of what I had seen of the way the golf industry had developed in Japan and America, the golfing position in the UK was undoubtedly going to change – and change quite quickly. All in all, I thought it was a very interesting prospect. I was intrigued.'

At that time, Wentworth was owned by AMEC whose two requirements of the sale were that it should be kept secret and done quickly. Bernerd began a reconnaissance, then sat down with his associates to determine how much the Club was worth. A figure approaching £20 million was agreed of which Chelsfield put up 60 per cent and Benlox, their partners, 40 per cent. It was settled within weeks and concluded in style, with Michael Broke, Chelsfield's Deputy Chairman, signing some documents in London at midday, taking a helicopter to Cheshire and signing more documents at midnight.

At the time, the price seemed a bargain for a property that stretched over 800 acres, had two thousand members, two golf courses with a third under construction, a swimming pool and tennis courts – and an enormous name in golf. Bernerd disagrees. 'We paid a record price for any golf establishment in the UK ,' he said. 'In fact, some people thought we had overpaid for it. Don't forget we bought a business for getting on for £20 million that had a turnover of £1 million annually and was making no money at all.'

Once the deal was announced, however, it quickly became clear that it was the sort of coup for which Bernerd had got his name in the property world. Within 24 hours a more lucrative offer for Wentworth from another company was received. Bigger and better offers from companies around the world started to roll in, from Australia, Japan, the Middle East, Europe. Every few days there was another approach. The temptation to cash in quickly was tremendous. In January 1989 Benlox wanted Chelsfield to sell out. They wanted a quick infusion of cash to pursue other interests.

'Chelsfield did not want to sell,' said Bernerd. 'The more we got involved, the more we liked it, so we bought them out. We gave them a profit of about £10 million. So effectively, our book costs jumped to £30 million.'

Bernerd's next manoeuvre was a master stroke. When in Japan on business, he had seen that shares in individual golf clubs were quoted on golfing stock exchanges and much sought after. He decided he would like to do the same at Wentworth. It was eighteen months before the idea was launched. It was simple. The Wentworth Club was valued at £80 million and 40 shares of £800,000 each were offered and quickly sold to corporate members such as The Savoy Group of hotels. The sum thus raised was £32 million. Chelsfield retained 60 per cent ownership yet had total control and recovered all its costs. It was what is known as a sweetheart deal. 'We weren't unhappy about it,' said Bernerd with typical British understatement. 'I was quite pleased.'

The third hole on the Edinburgh course with an approach shot to an elevated green

Other developments in golf may follow but what Bernerd has done is to define Wentworth in his own mind as a golf and country club of international standing rather than just a local community with additional sports facilities.

'What I have tried to explain to Club Members all along is that if you do not pay very much and have a large staff working for you (greenkeepers, kitchen staff, waiters, doormen) and you have not the money to pay them because you have not got the facilities working properly, who suffers? The Members.

'Since we purchased Wentworth the turnover has gone up five or six times and the whole place has changed. The Club is busy and well attended. It has come back as a living thing. The Members are getting good quality. They are being provided with far higher standards than they ever aspired to before. We are,' says Chairman Elliott Bernerd, 'giving the Members the quality they deserve.'

Future Plans

RENTON LAIDLAW

Elliott Bernerd, Chairman of Chelsfield, the company that had bought Wentworth, always knew the man he wanted to run that side of the company business. His name was Willy Bauer. Although at first he seemed an unlikely choice because of his lifetime association with 5-Star hotels rather than golf clubs, Bernerd knew he was the man for a job which, in time, will involve much more than supervising the running of the Wentworth Club. Although Willy Bauer, Chief Executive of Wentworth Group Holdings, has an office at Wentworth at the moment, it is more than possible that he will eventually run the Group from a London base. Significantly, he has not moved from his Dulwich home to the Wentworth estate despite the fact that it is the Wentworth Club which commands his whole attention at the moment.

It is as well to realize the situation at Wentworth. Chelsfield bought the Club from AMEC for £20 million and then sold off 40 per cent thereby not only recouping quickly the initial outlay but making a profit into the bargain. Chelsfield Chairman Bernerd then formed the self-supporting Wentworth Group Holdings to run his new golf venture which he wanted Willy Bauer to head. It is this newly formed company which generates, without Chelsfield assistance, the money that permits the continuing and necessary improvement and refurbishment including, with the help of a substantial long-term bank

Architect's drawing of the new clubhouse – north west elevation

loan, the rebuilding in traditional style of the castellated clubhouse.

The original plan drawn up by Arup Associates envisaged demolishing the old house that had served as the clubhouse since the 1920s to replace it with an ultramodern building at a cost of between £25 million and £30 million. Closer examination of the situation prompted Willy Bauer, at the eleventh hour, to ask for the whole project to be re-evaluated. The result was the abandonment of the grandiose scheme. It was replaced by one which envisaged completely gutting the clubhouse to enable the interior to be elegantly refurbished while retaining and improving the original exterior. This bold decision not only pleased the existing members of the Club – Bauer had quickly detected a groundswell of dissatisfaction with the plan for a modern clubhouse – but elicited a considerable saving. The new home of the Wentworth Club cost just £10 million.

If, five years ago, you had suggested to Willy Bauer that he would be running a golf club, even a prestigious one like Wentworth, he would not have taken you seriously. After all, the background of the 55-year-old German from Stuttgart was in top hotel management. He had worked in Lausanne and Geneva as well as in France, improving his French. Later, he moved to London to extend further his hotel experience and improve his English. From the Grand at Eastbourne he moved to the Hilton when it opened in Park Lane. He had spells with Grand Metropolitan and Trust Houses before and after it was taken over by Forte.

Back in London, he supervised, in his role as General Manager, the complete refurbishment of the Hyde Park Hotel, still one of the jewels in the Forte chain. Later, he took over as Director and General Manager at the Grosvenor House Hotel on Park Lane before moving to The Savoy in 1981. Ironically, years before when he had applied for a job as a waiter at The Savoy he had been turned down! His duties with The Savoy Group involved much more than day-to-day business at a hotel well known worldwide for its style and friendliness. He supervised the company's investment in Wilton's Restaurant in Jermyn Street and was closely involved when the Lygon Arms at Broadway became part of The Savoy Group.

When the executive head-hunters called in by Bernerd in 1988

Willy Bauer, Chief Executive Wentworth Club

Architect's drawing of the new clubhouse – north east elevation

made their first approach to Bauer, he told them to forget it – in the most diplomatic way, of course. He had little experience in golf. Moreover, running a golf club was hardly his idea of the obvious next step in his career of nearly 30 years in top class hotel administration.

Bauer had never met Elliott Bernerd but when he and Wentworth's new owner sat down in the Chelsfield headquarters in Brook Street there was immediate chemistry between them. Bauer, impressed by the offer, joined the Wentworth Club in 1989.

This was not an easy time. He always knew that settling in would demand considerable tact. The take-over had been achieved with almost undue haste and he knew the existing membership were apprehensive about the motives behind the take-over. Would they see him as the man sent in to tidy up things for a quick sale? Those who did, had not realized that Bauer would never have accepted the Wentworth job had there been any suggestion that Bernerd had bought the Club simply to make a quick killing. He had not.

Willy Bauer saw the wisdom of having Richard Doyle-Davidson, the former Club Secretary, by his side, a man who had done so much for the Club. Doyle-Davidson was convinced that there really was an important role for him in Bauer's masterplan – the rebuilding of the relationship between the new management, the members and the staff. Bauer, relating matters to his hotel background, saw the Wentworth members as the regular and valued customers of any

(Right and opposite)
Artist's impression of two rooms in the new clubhouse

hotel. The Club members were the vital heart of the new operation. He listened to their views and gave them his support. The Wentworth membership, while appreciating that things had changed forever, became less anxious about their future in the modernized and upgraded Club.

If the members were the one major asset at Bauer's disposal, he had three and a half additional assets of some importance – the courses which needed to be given more care and attention. With the help of the PGA European Tour, whose offices had been moved to Wentworth in 1981, he signed up Course Superintendent Chris Kennedy from Haggs Castle to head an enlarged greenkeeping staff. To run the clubhouse, he needed a keen golfer with a proper training in the food and beverage trade. Keith Williams, operating then at the Capital Hotel in Knightsbridge, seemed just the man. Williams jumped at the chance to join Bauer whom he had met socially during Bauer's time at the nearby Hyde Park Hotel.

Initially, Robbie James replaced Richard Doyle-Davidson as Club Secretary on the new Wentworth team but later, when he moved to the Walton Heath Golf Club, Bauer replaced him with Niall Flanagan who had just the right grounding in golf – he came from the Southern Region of the PGA. Flanagan, given the new title of Club Administrator under Keith Williams's authority, fitted in well.

With Bauer spending more and more time on the development

of the new clubhouse, he left Williams and Flanagan to manage Club affairs. Original Special Projects Manager Jose Borges who has now moved on, Director of Finance David Oakley and Willy Bauer positioned themselves in the new Wentworth Group Holdings offices alongside Bernard Gallacher's shop in a building scheduled for demolition.

In the new clubhouse, Gallacher's shop and the Group's offices are integrated into the design so that the building they now share can

Getting the courses back in shape

As part of a commitment to excellence at Wentworth, almost £1.5 million has been spent on improving the golf courses in the past three years – and it shows.

In 1990 when the Club's Course Manager Chris Kennedy arrived from Haggs Castle in Scotland, the courses – especially the West – were all showing visible signs of the wear and tear caused not only by two hot summers of drought conditions but also the lack of capital expenditure on course maintenance. The courses are built on a raft of Bagshot sand and gravel through which any nutrition quickly drains. There had been a lack of foliar feeding, the courses had not been aerated properly and the sun and wind had dried the grass on fairways lacking water because of the prolonged dry spell. The watering system that was installed after Richard Doyle-Davidson's arrival in the late 1970s covered only tees and greens. By 1993, however, the courses had improved beyond all recognition.

Kennedy's first job was to hollow core the fairways and dress them with a fertilizer which, over a period, released much needed nutrients into soil which had been virtually dormant. That was easy enough to do but much more was needed and the necessary capital was borrowed to bring Wentworth's courses back to prime condition. The company spent £400,000 on new machinery, including sophisticated mowers, that would help greenkeeping staff keep the West course in 'professional tournament' condition all year and not merely for the week of whatever tournament was being staged. More importantly, a decision was taken to replace the existing watering system with a new state-

of-the-art facility that would cover tees, greens, fairways and even rough on the West and Edinburgh courses as well as service, to a lesser extent, the East.

The Toro System 8000 is, perhaps, more accurately described as an irrigation and water conservancy system because the sprinklers operate only when necessary. If it starts to rain while the sprinklers are on, the computer turns them off! To make it all work there had to be water, of course. Thames Water solved the irrigation problem by laying on water from beyond the A30 through a specially constructed main. This in turn was connected to 11 miles of piping around the courses, some of it 2 inches in diameter and some 10 inches in diameter.

Three weather stations were built – essentially, one for each of Wentworth's three courses. These are connected to a sophisticated computer which controls, to the second, when water is pumped through to the course. An ingenious computer program determines which of the many sprinkler heads to activate and on which course. There are 600 on the West course alone. Water charges are £2,000 a month at Wentworth on average but careful, sensible use of water has transformed the Burma Road.

In these days of ecological awareness, it is not surprising that Wentworth is 'green'. Most of the fertilizers used on the courses are organic which helps the conservation and protection of the deer, badgers, foxes and other animals, as well as the many species of birds, that make the Wentworth Estate their home. In addition, the use of organic fertilizers is an added safeguard for the many pets kept by house owners.

The Club has embarked, too, on a policy geared to restoring Colt's masterpieces to their original glory. This has meant redesigning many of the fairway and greenside bunkers and revetting the banks to make be demolished to make way for an extension of the Club's leisure facilities in the future.

On that beautifully warm day in the autumn of 1989 when Willy Bauer drove down the A3 towards Wentworth with his wife, Zdenka, they were a little nervous about what lay ahead and apprehensive about the reception they would receive, it was hardly surprising. They were moving out of an environment they knew intimately into one in which they would necessarily be learning as they went along. Yet there

recovery from them more difficult. Fairways have been shaped, rough graded to what Kennedy calls 'a fair standard' and extensive landscaping has made everything look even better than it did before.

Kennedy, with the advice of Club Professional Bernard Gallacher, is trying to reach a point where the West and East courses offer the same degree of difficulty as designer Colt originally intended. This is more difficult than might at first be imagined. In professional events, big hitters such as Greg Norman have been known to hit the par 5 571-yard seventeenth hole with a massive drive around the dogleg followed by a 7-iron! Colt never envisaged that!

While the newest of the three courses – the Edinburgh – has bent fescue heathland grass throughout, the West and East have bent fescue only on the fairways. The tees and greens are poanna, or annual meadow grass, with just a suspicion of bent. While bent

fescue remains the same throughout the year, the meadow grass, which provides excellent putting surfaces, is winter dormant. Rhododendrons and azaleas have been planted to provide, in time, additional colour to the course. Dwarf specimen firs, beech and oak have been planted too, and the natural heather is being restored to the rough.

Over 80,000 rounds are played on the three courses throughout the year and, like the Old course at St Andrews, the East, West and Edinburgh are all closed for play one month every year for essential maintenance, a luxury many clubs cannot afford.

Wentworth's courses, so natural in their layout, are very different from American courses which require much closer management. However, Kennedy and his team have been chosen not merely for their expertise but also for their dedication to excellence which matches the Wentworth image.

The Wentworth sprinkler system is state-of-the-art

Five-star service
at the nineteenth!

From the day in March 1990 when Keith Williams arrived to take over as General Manager of the new style Wentworth, he was determined to maintain, indeed, accelerate, the move to upgrade all clubhouse standards.

Work had already begun on the rebuilding and refurbishment programme which included installing a fireplace from a chateau in France discovered by the interior designers, the RPW Partnership headed by Patrick Reardon. Traditional period pieces were collected over the months from antique outlets to ensure the ambiance of the clubhouse was just right. The Burma Bar, so much a feature of the old clubhouse, is still there but bigger and better than ever and with spikeproof carpets to allow those coming straight off the course to have a quick drink before changing.

The locker rooms are designed and furnished to the highest standard, reminding one of those in the finest of America's most fashionable clubs – and planning permission has already been passed for a quite separate leisure centre with heated indoor pool, gymnasium and aerobics room to be linked to the existing tennis pavilion. The new clubhouse has, like the old one, a Ryder Cup room, a Curtis Cup room, a Haliburton room for smaller functions plus a new Masters room.

'From day one,' says Keith Williams, 'I was well aware that everyone at Wentworth was working towards making it the finest golf and country club in Europe and among the finest in the world, not just in the high standard of clubhouse fittings and course facilities but also in the quality of food served and the service provided by the 120-strong staff. Prior to my arrival in 1990, an English chef, Norman Cook, had been employed to transform the hitherto acceptable standard of golf club fare into the highest quality English cuisine and to achieve the level of excellence to which the Club would aspire to in every other sphere in the future.

'And now, in readiness for the move into the refurbished clubhouse, we are pleased to have Ian McAndrew with us.'

Ian McAndrew had gained much experience at the Dorchester, owned his own restaurant for a time at Canterbury and is the author of two best selling cookery books. All week the always friendly staff are kept busy serving breakfasts, lunches and dinners from a menu that includes many Wentworth specialities.

Today, the membership from all categories is around 3,000 of which 1,500 are golfing members. That is not an unreasonable number for a club with three courses. It is a comfortable number to cope with as the Club heads confidently towards the year 2000.

For the moment, every member of staff is simply concentrating on settling into a new era in a new home designed not only with the golfer's needs very much in mind but with the requirements of every member in mind as well.

Chef Ian McAndrew with two of Wentworth's culinary delights

*Richard Doyle-Davidson welcomes
Zdenka and Willy Bauer to Wentworth
in August 1989*

really was never any doubt that Bernerd had chosen wisely. Bauer has
always enjoyed a challenge. The Wentworth Chief Executive readily
admits that his initial anxiety about missing the luxury hotel environment in central London has proved groundless. He has extensively
used his knowledge of running hotels to help him set new standards
at Wentworth but he has learned much, too, about the business and
commercial side, not least from Bernerd, the man who was always
determined to have him on his team.

*Keith Williams, General Manager,
with Chris Kennedy, Course Manager
and Niall Flanagan,
Club Administrator*

Getting the corporate image right

When Zdenka Beck was appointed Director of Marketing and Public Relations for the Wentworth Club by Elliott Bernerd, one of her first tasks was to work on a new design strategy which would effectively reflect the Club's new, more diverse image without destroying the important reputation it had as one of Britain's leading golf clubs. Changes there were going to be. However, the new management team realized that it was as important to consolidate 70 years of golfing history as it was to expand the tennis facilities and provide leisure and social facilities of the highest standard.

She knew the task had to be handled diplomatically. The existing members were not well-disposed to change of any kind. For instance, they were rather attached to the Club's existing if somewhat outdated motif – a reproduction of the castellated clubhouse. This had been introduced fifteen years earlier by Club Professional Bernard Gallacher for marketing purposes. Zdenka wanted a more sophisticated, up-market, 1990s motif for a club which by the turn of the century would again be a trendsetter, a prime example of all that is best in golf and country club development.

The new design not only had to marry the past with the future, it had to be adaptable. It would be used discreetly across a wide range of products from Club stationery to crockery and applied to the extensive range of branded merchandise in Gallacher's well stocked shop. Zdenka rationalized the Wentworth stationery by reducing the 98 pieces of paper that used the Club logo

to 29 and made a considerable cost saving.

The development of the new logo and its introduction was, by necessity, done in stages. This was as much for financial reasons – there were not unlimited funds – as to minimize the antagonism caused to those members opposed to its introduction.

Zdenka decided that Wentworth's new colours which would be used in the logo should be green – British Racing Green seemed appropriate – and terracotta. She and the Committee felt that this combination symbolized the friendliness of the Club.

Several companies were approached to produce designs. The contract went to Raymond Loewy International who have been leaders in this field for 60 years. Among their clients are Shell International, Coutts and Coca Cola for whom they designed the now famous bottle in 1947. The company produced eight designs. All of them complied with the Club's requirement that the new logo should be easy to apply to a wide range of Club related items, from golf balls to dining room menus and blazer buttons. Moreover, it was essential that the new logo should be easier to embroider on clothing than the old one had been. The proposed designs all complied with this requirement as well.

The design that was eventually chosen is ideal. It meets the Club's criteria and symbolizes its pride in 70 years of golfing tradition while at the same time signifying its preparedness to move confidently into the 21st century. It is a traditional shield (delineated on the right but not the left to avoid comparison with school shields) with a distinctive, indeed, unique 'W' inset. It is topped by crenellations which are reminiscent of both the old logo and the redesigned clubhouse, its exterior

Zdenka Beck discusses the poster for the Ascot ball with artist Ron Wyatt and Eileen Potter

(Opposite) The Club has two ties, one for members (right) and the other for visitors

rebuilt in its original style. The shield is split vertically , one half in British Racing Green and the other in terracotta, the Club's new colours.

Besides supervising the design of a new logo, Prague-born Zdenka has other important roles included motivating the staff – something she had done excellently in her role as Sales Manager at The Savoy – and expanding the social aspect of the Club, especially on the female side. She started a highly successful aerobics class. She organized fashion shows and staged talks on dress design and make-up. She helped the Social Committee with the Ascot, Easter, Christmas and New Year Balls and ran a tennis tournament with a distinctive American theme. She even arranged for singers from the Royal Opera House to come and sing for members in a reciprocal deal which gave the Royal Opera House a golf day at the Club. And she persuaded Sotheby's to hold an antique roadshow and golfing memorabilia exhibition in the ballroom. In addition, she revived and expanded the Club Newsletter, initially with the help of journalist John Spencer, giving more space to those branches of Club activity not concerned with golf. So far, all these duties have prevented her from playing golf although she has promised to squeeze lessons on to her busy agenda.

Scholarships

RENTON LAIDLAW

*Tom Haliburton always took a great
interest in the youngsters at Wentworth*

Wentworth is Europe's most successful golf club in
a corporate sense but it is also unique in what it
does to encourage and develop the talent of the
next generation of golfers. In 1991 Elliott Bernerd,
Chairman of the Wentworth Club, launched a
£200,000 five year initiative to guide and manage the more talented
youngsters in both golf and tennis by offering coaching scholarships.
While Wentworth, with its three championship courses and nine hole

short course, is best known internationally for golf, the Club also boasts a thriving tennis section operating from its own custom-built clubhouse that overlooks a complex with a variety of surfaces – Greenset Supreme, all-weather courts, French clay courts (unique in Britain) and traditional grass courts. Only at Wentworth can British tennis players experience all the surfaces used in Grand Slam tennis around the world, a facility which helps develop true all-round players.

Wentworth's golfers may look forward each year to the Volvo PGA Championship and the Toyota World Match-play Championship but the Club's tennis players have welcomed top stars in their sport, too – Ivan Lendl and Martina Navratilova among them.

The Scholarship schemes, financed jointly by the Club and the Bernerd Foundation and run by a separate Board of Trustees, has three main aims: firstly, to promote and encourage the very best in junior golf and tennis in the United Kingdom; secondly, to bring Wentworth's own juniors into contact with the best golf and tennis juniors in the country; and thirdly, to underline the Club's commitment to junior golf and tennis. In this respect, the Club is fortunate in having Bernard Gallacher as golf Professional. The Ryder Cup Captain may have an impressive reputation as a tournament player but he is also one of the game's most respected coaches.

Tennis, too, is well served at Wentworth. The Club's Director of Tennis is Rohun Beven whose ten years experience of coaching has included taking Britain's Under-18 team to the World Junior Championship in Miami in 1983. He has also travelled to Australia and America while working with Sara Gomer and Julie Salmon.

The aim of the Tennis Scholarships is not only to give the youngsters a very sound grounding in all the technical aspects of the game but also to concentrate on improving their fitness as well as their psychological approach to the game. Open annually to six promising youngsters aged eight years and up from the local area, the Tennis Scholarships incorporate group coaching and one-to-one teaching which can be on a weekly or a daily basis according to the player's ability, commitment and availability between school studies. One of the Scholarship Trustees, Jo Ellen Grzyb, assists the youngsters in developing higher playing standards by teaching them how to cope mentally with the stresses and strains of the game.

The Golf Scholarships, which benefit twelve youngsters a year, is tied in with the Golf Foundation's Nationwide Age Group Championships. The seven winners of the Weetabix sponsored age Group Championship competitions are given first choice to join the Wentworth scheme. The popular Age Group tournaments are divided into seven categories – four for boys aged twelve, thirteen, fourteen and fifteen and three for girls aged thirteen, fourteen and fifteen. Thousands enter each year. The complement is made up of juniors from the local Club and, as a later refinement to the original concept,

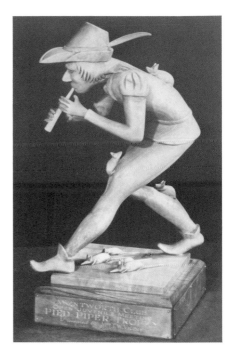

The Club's Pied Piper *trophy for the winner of the annual Open Juvenile meeting, was presented by Mrs Pat Vigers*

Prince Edward (above) with the winner of the 1992 Golden Putter and Prince Andrew (right) deep in discussion with Willy Bauer

six young golfers with talent who for one reason or another are unable to belong to a club.

A big bonus for the golfing Scholarship winners is the week's intensive coaching from Club Professional Gallacher. His aim has always been to improve the youngsters' technique and teach the value of practising properly. Spending hours on the range can be a total waste of time if you are practising the wrong thing. In those circumstance, it is possible to aggravate a fault instead of eradicating it.

'We have some great young golfers in the United Kingdom today,' says Gallacher, 'and with so much more talent around as more and more youngsters are introduced to the game, it is important to instill the right kind of attitude in them from an early age. Any youngster aiming to make it to the top needs more than ability. He or she needs to know how to play through those periods when nothing seems to go right.'

After the week's intensive coaching, the young golfers progress throughout the year is carefully monitored by Gallacher and his team of well trained assistants. Youngsters keen to return for refresher courses are encouraged to do so. By initiating the two carefully financed schemes, Wentworth Club hopes not only to play a part in giving youngsters with obvious potential encouragement to work hard at their chosen sport, but also to help produce the young men and women who will be the natural successors to Britain's respected world stars in golf – Nick Faldo and Laura Davies.

If the Club's golf programme is geared to developing the playing skills of a future Open champion or a future British Ladies' Open champion, the long-term aim of the tennis scheme is to produce badly needed Wimbledon champions. It will, of course, take time.

The Scholarship schemes are not the only link Wentworth has with junior golf. The Club annually hosts the Duke of Edinburgh's Award Scheme Young Golfers Challenge Final – appropriately on the Edinburgh course. Over 500 young golfers who are Duke of Edinburgh Award holders take part in the competition aimed, like the Scholarship schemes, at making young people more aware of the challenge, self-discipline and skills of golf. Unlike the Scholarships, however, the age range of those allowed and encouraged to participate in the Duke's golf event is fourteen to 25. It is only open to those

Eddie Shah, a Director, shareholder and generous benefactor of the Golf and Tennis Scholarships

(Left) Rohun Beven, in charge of Wentworth's thriving tennis section, works with younger players

(Left) In all his years as Club Professional, leading player and Ryder Cup Captain, Bernard Gallacher has always found the time to instruct juniors

golfers who have earned a Duke of Edinburgh's Award that specifically recognizes endurance, resilience, bravery and initiative in a broad range of activities likely to develop leadership qualities. The Young Golfers Challenge Final is organized by Eric Worrall, Deputy Director of the Duke of Edinburgh's Award Scheme, with his golf projects director, Jimmy Jewell. Close on 100 captains of industry support the Duke's competition and have raised over £100,000 to promote and help run the event.

The two junior oriented events at Wentworth plus the Club's fund raising activities for the continuing work of the Golf Foundation which, through school coaching, introduced thousands of youngsters to the game each year, are just a few of the ways in which the Club helps and encourages the younger generation to improve its golf and tennis. Maybe one day a Wentworth youngster will end up Open champion or take a Wimbledon title. That would be the ultimate reward for the dedicated work put in by Wentworth's top coaches Bernard Gallacher and Rohun Beven to make the Scholarship scheme work.

Blind golfers take on the West course

Golf may seem to be a very self indulgent pastime but the game has always been closely involved with charity, not least at Wentworth. The charities that have been supported by the Club by fund raising events are wide ranging, from those supporting the profoundly deaf to cancer research, from organizations dedicated to helping seriously disturbed youngsters to those who train guide dogs for the blind.

One of the most inspiring tournaments occurred in 1991 when teams of British and American blind players staged their own Ryder Cup. Organized by the RNIB, the two day competition provided those involved with a unique appreciation of the wonderful sensitivity, skill and sheer enjoyment experienced by unsighted golfers. The professionals present, Nick Faldo, Sandy Lyle and Ronan Rafferty, all found it 'a humbling experience'.

Other Charity days at Wentworth include the Bobby Charlton Classic, the Harry Carpenter competition for the National Association of Boys Clubs and Children Say, an organization which provides funds for operations and treatment unavailable on the NHS for children born without ears or with hearing difficulties.

Each unsighted golfer had a caddie who lined up the shots and assisted with the putting. For the Wentworth Tournament the RNIB produced braille maps of each hole on the course

Postscript

DICK TAYLOR

In the winter of 1964 I made the mistake of scheduling, too early, the tournaments I planned to cover for the year. In July these included the Open followed immediately by the World Seniors Professional Championship. That meant almost seven months of thinking excitedly about a dream that was to come true: I was going to see both the Old course at St Andrews and Wentworth under competitive conditions. Both had been high on my fantasy list for years because of the history and fame that surrounded these bastions of 'real' golf.

Having been imbued with the importance of history at an early age by an aunt who taught the subject and having made the delightful discovery of how interesting mankind's progress has been, I eventually majored in history in college. This predilection has been both a blessing and a disadvantage in my career. When interviewing Ben Hogan each spring in the 1950s, I was in such awe of this historical figure that he must have though me a blithering idiot.

These farces took place at another famed golf course, Seminole near Palm Beach, Florida during the twelve years I presided over the sports sections of the *Palm Beach Post*. Nightly, I would strip wire service copy from machines clattering out international sports news and, nightly, I would daydream after the paper's sports section had been 'put to bed'.

The datelines and the events captured one's imagination: Wimbledon, Forest Hills, Le Mans, Indy 500, Kitzbuhel, Lake Placid and the Winter Olympics, Tokyo and Rome and the Summer Olympics, the Rose Bowl and White City Stadium. The list seemed endless but golf was my game. There was a magical quality about editing stories from St Andrews, Pebble Beach, Portmarnock, Baltusrol, Royal Melbourne and Wentworth, a famous sextet of golfing venues drenched in history and histrionics.

It has been my great fortune as editor of *Golf World USA* from 1962 to 1989 and as a syndicated columnist for five magazines in three countries since then, to visit all those clubs and more. But in the summer of 1964 those pleasures were yet to come.

Wentworth had first caught my attention in October 1953 during two desperate days of Ryder Cup play. In those days, the wire services would clang out bulletins with match by match results rather than wait until day's end for a general story. The United States and Great Britain were locked in a titanic struggle in the closing singles after a first day blowout in which Great Britain lost three of the four foursomes to the Americans. It was almost as exciting for me to watch the match unfold on a teletype machine in Florida as it would have been had I been there in person. The contestants extolled the Burma Road, an appellation easily indentifiable as Wentworth from anywhere in the world.

Later that year, I was at the nearby Boca Raton Club for an event. Snead held forth there following the retirement of legendary 'Silver Scot' Tommy Armour . He was his usual blunt self about the Ryder Cup, prefacing his singles loss with a reminder that he and Mangrum had 'whomped up' on Eric Brown and John Panton 8 and 7 in foursomes. As for the singles upset: 'You've heard of the Postage Stamp hole at Troon? Well, that West course at Wentworth is a whole post office!' Praise indeed from Snead!

The usual history inquisitive light bulb lit up in my brain. I knew that Harry S Colt was the main man in its design with business partners Charles H Alison and John Stanton Fleming Morrison (who sounds like a law office) . Colt was a very inventive and influential architect. If Donald Ross was the father of American architecture, then Colt's body of work in the Colonies made him a close relative. Just as Alister Mackenzie, helped by Bobby Jones, had changed philosophies on course design with Augusta National Golf Club, so Colt was equally influential with Wentworth.

Wentworthians did get to see Hogan in 1956 when the Canada Cup (now the World Cup) imported an international cast for a June celebration of the sport. However, I was again confined to my Florida office. That meant I missed watching Gary Player, a 20-year-old whiz from South Africa who had astounded all in a five round event at Sunningdale when he returned 70, 64, 64, 72, 68 – 338 over two courses. Cup major-domo Fred Corcoran extolled 'the boy' as a wonder in the mould of Jones, Hagen and Sarazen at the same age.

'It is not going to be a runaway for the US,' warned Fred, 'even with Hogan and Snead as representatives. The South Africans will challenge with Bobby Locke teaming with his protege Gary Player.'

Fred was half right. South Africa was second to the United States but a distant fourteen shots away.

Again, the Virginia Water, Surrey, England wire service dateline captivated me, as well as a quirky timetable. The play was Sunday through Tuesday with a double round on the final day which Hogan hated. One story crossing my desk explained that fifteen thousand spectators were made Wentworth members on the Sunday to get around what we call 'blue laws' in America because of pious church goers. The cost of one day membership was ten shillings. How I wished I was there.

Such distant venues were beyond my ken until I made my first transatlantic trip in 1964. First, I saw Tony Lema beat back Jack Nicklaus at the Open, then came the World Seniors match at Wentworth, sponsored by Ronald Teacher, boss of Teachers whisky, which had an almost garden-party atmosphere. It was Sam Snead versus Syd Scott. The cast stayed in a hotel in Maidenhead and we were all grandly transported to the famous club in Daimlers! This was Wentworth style!

After the Ryder Cup, Snead said that Wentworth with its tennis courts and swimming pool was more like an American country club than an English golf club. He was wrong. No American club uses the estate of a former stately home for its golf courses. Nowhere do we have rhododendrons the size of horses heads bobbing in the wind, and there are but few American clubhouses as richly appointed as the one that has just been refurbished in an appropriately grand manner by the folks at Wentworth.

One of my home clubs is Pinehurst Country Club, located in North Carolina's Sandhills. This was Donald Ross's home base where revered Pinehurst Number Two is a golfing Mecca. With sandy subsoil, rolling terrain and pine forest, Pinehurst is something akin to the Surrey area courses. Except that instead of the Wentworth silver birches and great oaks Pinehurst has firs. But the love of the game is the same.

Snead made a travesty of the one day, 36 hole match with a morning 37 and 32 – 69 to be five up before a sumptuous luncheon. It ended 7 and 6. Sam had said he had not had time to experiment with the small ball so would play the larger version but once on the first tee he changed his mind and was brilliant. Rain plagued the day and a hardy crowd of fifteen hundred had vanished by afternoon play.

My stay was all too brief but along came the Piccadilly World Match-play Championship (now the Toyota) and I was back at Wentworth. There is one vibrant memory from one of those events. A young Seve Ballesteros had one of his 'parking lot' rounds to defeat machine-like Hale Irwin. 'If he plays like that when he comes to America,' said an agitated Irwin afterwards, 'he won't last a month!'

I last visited Wentworth during the Walker Cup at Sunningdale in 1987. The Volvo PGA Championship was being staged at about the same time and it became an irresistible urge to spend at least one day with this *grande dame* of golf. Sky boxes surrounded the eighteenth green, hospitality tents dotted the landscape and commercial bunting flapped in the wind. It was all so different from the way it had looked on my first visit in 1964. It was still beautiful but it is the Wentworth of 30 years ago – a sedate but sensuous seductress – that I prefer to remember. No wonder they call it *wonderful* Wentworth.

The seventh on the West at Wentworth – at its best in the autumn

Index

ACKNOWLEDGEMENTS

The following writers contributed to the book:

Michael Britten *(Sunday Mirror)*
Colin Callander *(Golf Monthly)*
Bruce Critchley
David Davies *(The Guardian)*
Peter Dobereiner
Bill Elliott *(The Star)*
Bob Ferrier
Tim Glover *(The Independent)*
Robert Green *(Golf World)*
John Hopkins *(The Times)*
John Ingham
Ramond Jacobs *(Glasgow Herald)*

Renton Laidlaw *(Evening Standard)*
Mitchell Platts
Chris Plumridge *(Sunday Telegraph)*
Gordon Richardson *(The News of the World)*
Dick Taylor *(Southern Links)*
Michael Williams *(The Daily Telegraph)*
John Whitbread *(Surrey Herald)*

The extract from *A Subaltern's Love Song*, on page 27, by John Betjeman is reproduced by kind permission of John Murray, publishers

PICTURE CREDITS

Every effort has been made to contact the copyright owners to seek their permission before reproducing the pictures in this book. Any error or omission in acknowledging ownership is regretted.

ACTION PHOTOS: 69 (bottom), 70 (bottom), 107, 108
ALLSPORT: 17 (debenture), 55 (bottom left), 66 (bottom), 67 (top), 70 (top), 81 (top), 104, 137, 151 (top & bottom); Howard Boylan 133; David Cannon 4 (frontispiece), 41 (bottom left), 53, 54, 55 (top), 56/57, 62, 63, 66 (top), 67 (bottom), 96, 111 (left), 117, 118, 122, 123, 130, 135, 140/141, 147, 149 (bottom), 150; Steve Munday 99, 109, 126, 136; Mike Powell 111 (right), 127; Anton Want 36, 41 (top right), 143 (top), 148
CHARLES BRISCOE-KNIGHT: 155 (top left & bottom left)
THE DUKE OF EDINBURGH'S AWARD: 9
DAVID ELEMENT: dust jacket front (butterfly)
BIRDIE GOLF: 52, 65 (bottom left)
COUNTRYSIDE IMAGES:
Frank V Blackburn 60 (bottom left)
FOX PHOTOS LTD: 75, 152
D W GARDNER: 20
GUARDIAN/MANCHESTER EVENING NEWS: 155 (top right)
JOHN HESELTINE: 49
IMG: 119 (top)
JOHN JACOBS GOLF ASSOCIATES: 59
LNA: 30 (bottom), 31

LADIES' GOLF UNION, St Andrews: 77, 79 (top left and top right)
JOHN C LONG: 38
TERRY O'NEILL: 11, 101
PGA EUROPEAN TOUR: 129
PGA RYDER CUP: 68
PHOTO COVERAGE: 35
K G PRINCE: 97
PHIL SHELDON: 119 (bottom)
RPW DESIGN PARTNERSHIP: 142 (bottom), 143 (bottom), 144, 145
SPORT & GENERAL: 94, 95, 102, 103
SURREY HERALD NEWS SERIES: 23, 37, 58, 60 (top), 61 (top left & right), 149 (top), 154 (left), 156
WENTWORTH CLUB: 13, 81 (bottom, presented by Molly Gourlay), 154 (right)
Courtesy GOLF WORLD: 30 (top left), 33, 42 (bottom left & bottom right), 43, 44, 45 (top left, top right & bottom right), 51 (Harry Colt), 69 (top), 73, 74, 78, 80, 88, 91, 92, 93
By kind permission of ELIZABETH HALIBURTON: 46
By permission of KNIGHT, FRANK & RUTLEY and WALTON & LEE: 16
By kind permission of TREVOR WILLIAMS: 39
Reproduced from *Illustrated History of Golf* by Alan Elliot and J A May, published by Hamlyn: 113
Reproduced from *Ryder Cup 1927-1989* by Michael Williams, published by Stanley Paul: 71
OTHERS (unknown): 21, 28, 29 (cartoon – source unknown), 72, 85, 86, 87 (top & bottom right), 153